£1·50

Ber

Cyprus

Front cover: Sanctuary of Apollo Ylatis

Right: Aphrodite in the Cyprus Museum

Panagia tou Araka – Lagoudera is home to one of the island's most celebrated frescoed churches (page 66)

Keryneia – The harbour is the most picturesque in Cyprus (page 81)

Cyprus Archaeological Museum •
A must-see in Nicosia, housing the island's finest collection of antiquities (page 31)

Stavrovouni Monastery
This historic landmark has magnificent views from its hill-top position (page 48)

Agia Napa Beaches of golden sand have made it one of the island's top destinations for sun seekers *(page 50)*

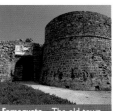

Famagusta The old town holds several architectural curiosities, including the impressive Venetian fortifications *(page 83)*

Rock of Aphrodite According to legend, Petra tou Romiou is the very spot where the goddess came ashore *(page 61)*

Akamas Peninsula The last great coastal wilderness of southern Cyprus is best explored off road *(page 77)*

Agios Neofytos Monastery The main highlight here is the lovely hermitage *(page 76)*

Kourion The ancient clifftop site is one of the island's archaeological highlights *(page 57)*

A PERFECT DAY

In Nicosia, start the day with a buffet breakfast at the Classic Hotel (see page 135), located near the Tripoli Bastion, just inside the impressive Venetian Walls that surround the Old City.

Cross over into Turkish Cypriot North Nicosia for a close-up view of the Selimiye Camii (Selimiye Mosque) and some of the nearby points of interest, such as Büyük Han (Great Inn) and Kumarcılar Hanı (Gamblers' Inn). If you think you have enough time, go in as far as bustling Atatürk Meydanı (Atatürk Square).

12 noon Scenic drive

Return to South Nicosia. Drive west out of the city on the B10, a scenic road that runs parallel to the UN Buffer Zone and becomes the B9 before going though Peristerona then curving southwards while climbing into the Troodos Mountains.

10.00am Stroll through Nicosia's Old City

Walk south to Plateia Eleftherias (Freedom Square) for a brief stroll among the restored buildings of the old Laiki Geitonia district, then head north along the pedestrianised shopping street of Odos Lidras (Ledra Street) to the Green Line crossing-point.

IN CYPRUS

4.00pm Past the island's highest mountain

Drive through the Troodos Mountains, passing Mount Olympos, then down to Pano Platres for a stroll through this pleasant mountain town.

10.00pm Homeward

Return to the A1. The motorway is generally very quiet at this time, so although it is the end of a long and busy day you should be able to return quickly and safely to your resort. If you're still up for a cocktail, make it Cyprus's own refreshingly sharp brandy sour.

6.00pm To the coast

Continue south, going downhill on the B8 through the Commandaria wine region, to join the A1 motorway at Limassol. Go east on the A1, and take the exit for the short drive to the coast at Zygi.

2.00pm At The Mill

Have lunch at The Mill restaurant in Kakopetria (see page 107), which serves great fresh trout and has a magnificent view over the restored Old Town. After lunch take a stroll through this fascinating part of Kakopetria.

8.00pm Seafood dinner in Zygi

Dine at one of Zygi's many fine seafood restaurants – a good choice is Markos (tel: 2433 3404), popular with Greek Cypriots and located at the seafront close to the old jetty.

28

97

43

CONTENTS

15

62

86

INTRODUCTION

Cyprus made its ancient fortune from copper, a chunk of history that's echoed today in one of the colours that make up the national flag. In modern times, Cyprus' greatest natural resource is sunshine, around 340 days a year. Yet 'Aphrodite's Island' has often been careless with the coastline that puts all that sunshine to good use. Many resorts are large and over-developed with little historical or cultural character, and the battle to preserve the remaining unspoiled coastline is being closely fought. But you don't have to delve far to begin to appreciate this island. A little way inland are countless old villages, a constellation of vineyards, and rugged mountain

ranges. The layers of a long and tangled history, from Stone Age peoples, through Greeks, Persians, Romans, Byzantines, Crusaders, Venetians, Turks and British, are there to be seen and felt.

Some of your finest memories are likely to be of a remarkably friendly and hospitable people – both Greek-Cypriot and Turkish-Cypriot. Considering their turbulent

An idyllic beach scene

and traumatic recent history, you have to marvel at the Cypriots' easy-going nature. This is, after all, an island that was invaded by Turkey and split in two in 1974. At a stroke, some 170,000 Greek Cypriots became refugees in their own country, and were forced to flee to the south of the island.

The remains of a Graeco-Roman temple at Kourion

The grape harvest

At the same time, around 30,000 Turkish Cypriots moved north. The island is still divided today, though since 2003 there has been greater freedom of movement across the border.

Although it's now much easier to visit the North (which only Turkey recognises as a separate republic), most travellers still choose the Greek-Cypriot South. But for those who do go across the line that separates the two parts of the island, the North offers a much less commercialised landscape, including some pristine beaches and more varieties of flora and fauna.

An Easy-Going People

Through all the turmoil, the Greek Cypriots have managed to retain a sunny disposition. The Greeks are by nature a friendly, hospitable people, but Cypriots seem to take this a stage further. Ask a couple harvesting grapes if you can take their photo, and they will not only strike a happy pose, but also gather a large bag of grapes for you to take home. Compliment a chef on the quality of his *sheftalia* at a taverna and chat to him about village life, and it's not impossible he will insist that lunch is on the house. Chat to an old man about Makarios and the EOKA days, and you'll notice 15 minutes later that he has left his family waiting in order to talk to a complete stranger. It is rare that a visitor leaves Cyprus without some tale of the people's generosity.

It is not a mere marketing gimmick that often at the end of a meal, coffee and a liqueur (even if it is the throat-charring *zivania*) is provided on the house. As you will probably hear said more than once, 'It is our custom'. You don't have to go to the most remote mountain village for such hospitality, but it is true that you are much less likely to find this warmth in the more obviously tourist-oriented watering holes.

This widespread cheerfulness is coupled with a dignity that shuns expansive Latin gestures. The British like to think that their presence on the island has been at least partly responsible, but the courtesy of Cypriots in general seems to be a more deeply ingrained quality.

The Lie of the Land

Tucked into the northeast corner of the Mediterranean between Turkish Anatolia and Syria, Cyprus is the Mediterranean's third largest island, after Sicily and Sardinia. Its land surface of 9,251 sq km (3,572 sq miles) sandwiches the broad Mesaoria Plain between two chains of mountains – the Pentadaktylos range in the northeast and the Troodos in the southwest. Three major rivers, which run dry in summer, originate in the Troodos Mountains: the Pediaios flowing east to Famagusta Bay, the Kargotis north to Morfou Bay, and the Kouris south to Episkopi. The highest peak is Mt Olympos, at 1,951m (6,401ft).

Population: Around 900,000 in the South, including 120,000 foreign residents; 265,000 in the North, including 150,000 post-1974 Turkish settlers.

Capital: Nicosia (Lefkosia/Lefkoşa): 225,000 in the Greek-Cypriot sector; 85,000 in the Turkish-Cypriot sector.

Major cities: South: Limassol (Lemesos; 190,000), Larnaka (80,000), Pafos (70,000). North: Famagusta (Ammochostos/Gazimağusa; 36,000), Morfou (Güzelyurt; 13,000), Keryneia (Girne; 30,000).

Troubled Relations

A more sombre note is struck when the matter of the divided island is raised. Greek-Cypriot refugees from the North react more with melancholy than anger. Nostalgically, restaurants and shops in Larnaka or Limassol may bear the names of their lost homes in Famagusta, Keryneia or Belapais. Some of that feeling has been tempered by the changes in recent years that have brought Greek and Turkish Cypriots into closer contact with each other, but it has not dissipated.

Sadly, because of its geographical position, Cyprus has been beset by unwelcome visitors throughout its history. Apart from attracting Phoenician and Assyrian pirates, and conquerors from Egypt, Persia, Greece and Turkey, Cyprus has been the easy prey of French crusaders and Venetian and Genoese merchants. The island was even a pawn in the last days of the British Empire.

Pano Lefkara in the Troodos foothills

The Island's Attractions

But for today's visitors, the traces of the past are a compelling reason for coming. There are ancient Greek and Roman ruins at Kourion and Salamis, splendid Roman mosaics at Pafos, the crusader castles of Kolossi and the Pentadakylos Mountains, and the Byzantine monasteries and churches of the Troodos Mountains.

Cyprus is a country of great natural beauty. While the resort beaches cater for holidaymakers happy to lie baking in serried ranks, the coastline, particularly of the Akamas Peninsula, has enough rugged cliffs and surf-beaten coves to appeal to the romantic individualist or rugged off-road biker. Inland, the Troodos Mountains are a wild and spectacularly verdant adventure of hairpin curves and restored forest. Sprinkled like forgotten gems in the landscape are tiny Byzantine churches, secrets known only to their parishioners for centuries. Today, 10 of these are on the Unesco protected list and no visit to Cyprus is complete without visiting at least one of them.

Meanwhile, in the plains of the interior, villages untouched by tourism nestle among olive groves and citrus orchards, and goats and sheep scamper among forgotten ancient ruins. Vineyards climb the sunny hillsides, cypress trees frame a somnolent abbey or the skeleton of an abandoned fortress, and rural Cypriot life continues at a gentle pace.

Greek names

Cyprus — at least the part under Greek-Cypriot control — is emphasizing its Greek character. Colonial-era names and spellings have given way to Greek names and updated transliterations from the Greek alphabet to the Latin. For instance, Paphos has been re-christened as Pafos and Ayia Napa as Agia Napa; more notable changes include Nicosia (now Lefkosia), Limassol (Lemesos), Famagusta (Ammochostos) and Kyrenia (Keryneia).

A BRIEF HISTORY

The first records of human presence in Cyprus seem to be those of a group who were nomads and hunters rather than permanently settled. Flint tools recently discovered offshore from the Akamas Peninsula and on Nissi Beach at Agia Napa prove that seafarers landed on Cyprus about 10000BC, a millennium earlier than previously thought. The bones of indigenous pygmy hippopotamuses and pygmy elephants (both now extinct) eaten by the mariners were also found. Tools and butchered animal bones found in a cave at Akrotiri on the south coast date from about 9000BC. Water wells found recently near Pafos are thought have been dug slightly later. The earliest traces of permanent settlers are dated at about 8000BC, with the most notable being the stone beehive-shaped dwellings at the tip of the Karpasia Peninsula and at the inland site of Choirokoitia, which date back to about 7000BC.

By 3500BC, copper was being mined in the Troodos foothills and Cyprus began to prosper as a trading centre, with goods coming in from Asia, Egypt, Crete, the Peloponnese and the Aegean Islands in exchange for Cypriot pottery, copperware and opium. After 1600BC, fortresses were built around the island, which suggests a period of conflict. Copper was sent to Egypt as protection money.

Greeks, Persians and Romans
Upheaval in the Peloponnese, caused variously by natural calamities and invasions from the north, drove Mycenaean Greeks east across the Mediterranean, and some settled in Cyprus. From 1200BC, they established city-kingdoms at Enkomi (Egkomi), replaced later by Salamis (near modern Famagusta), Kition (now Larnaka), Kourion, Palaia Pafos (Kouklia), Soloi and Lapithos. The island acquired the pre-

dominantly Greek identity it was never entirely to relinquish. Temples presided over by Aphrodite, the goddess of love and fertility, were erected near smelting workshops.

As the Persian Empire spread across the eastern Mediterranean in the 6th century BC, Cyprus, along with other Greek islands, was annexed. In 499BC it joined the Ionian Greek revolt but, after heroic resistance, notably during the siege of Palaia Pafos, was crushed by the Persians the next year.

In 333BC, Alexander the Great ended Persian dominance in the eastern Mediterranean and placed Cyprus under Macedonian rule. After his death in 323BC, the island was a battleground as his generals fought over the succession, flattening many ancient cities in the process. By 299BC, Ptolemy I emerged the victor, the city-kingdoms disappeared and Cyprus became part of the Hellenistic state of Egypt. The Ptolemies ruled for 250 years until the Romans, on a pretext that the island was harbouring pirates, annexed it in 58BC to their province of Cilicia (southern Turkey).

In 47BC, Julius Caesar made a present of Cyprus to Cleopatra, the last ruler of the Ptolemaic dynasty. After her suicide, Augustus took it back for the Romans and let King Herod of Judaea farm out the Cypriot copper mines to Jewish entrepreneurs.

Replica mosaic of *Leda and the Swan* at Kouklia *(see page 75)*

Detail of a terracotta figurine dating from the 5th century BC

The Byzantine Era

Despite the apostle Paul's mission to Cyprus in AD45, the islanders continued in their attachment to the cults of Aphrodite and, with the growth of highly prized vineyards, the wine god Dionysos. Only in the 4th century, as Christianity took a hold on the Roman leadership, did churches and monasteries begin to spring up across Cyprus. In AD330, the mother of the Roman emperor Constantine, Helena, is said to have visited the island and founded the great Stavrovouni Monastery.

Priests wielded considerable power over everyday life, defending peasants against tax collectors, but also demanding unquestioning allegiance. In 488, the archbishop of Cyprus gained total control over the island's spiritual affairs and began to carry a royal sceptre rather than a pastoral staff, wore a cloak of imperial purple and signed his name in imperial red ink – rights that the archbishops retain to this day.

With the Byzantine Empire weak from its war against Persia, the Arabs took the opportunity to cross over to Cyprus in 649 with a fleet of 1,500 ships. Salamis (now Constantia) was left in such ruins that it never recovered; the raid continued across the island until news of an approaching Byzantine fleet prompted retreat.

Four years later, in a move that foreshadowed events of the 20th century, the Arabs staged a second invasion and left a garrison of 12,000 men, encouraging Muslim immigration to establish a foothold on the island. The Byzantines and the Muslim Caliphate subsequently agreed to neutralise Cyprus – there would be no military bases, though ports could be used for re-fitting the navy – and also to share tax revenues. Over the next 300 years, Muslims and Christians engaged in offshore battles and launched raids against each other, but lived side by side.

The Crusades

During the time of the Crusades, Cyprus became a key strategic post for Byzantine interests in Syria and Palestine. The governor organised protection for pilgrims to the Holy Land and supervised the rebuilding of Jerusalem's Church of the Holy Sepulchre and fortifications for its Christian Quarter. The invasion of Ottoman Turks in Anatolia and the Levant after 1071 threat-ened communications with Constantinople, but Cyprus was still able to supply food to soldiers of the First Crusade in 1097 and even pro-vided refuge for defeated Muslim princes.

A Stavrovouni mosaic depicts Byzantine-era Christianity

New trade developed with Venice and the young Crusader states on the mainland. However, the Turks' conquest of Anatolia in 1176 isolated Cyprus from the Byzantine government. Isaac Comnenos, a junior member of the imperial family, felt free to make himself the despotic 'Emperor' of Cyprus, using Sicilian mercenaries to fight off the Byzantine fleet.

Asset stripper

Although King Richard deposed the 'emperor' Comnenos, he stripped the island of all its money to pay for his expedition to the Holy Land, and Greeks were denied any governing role. They were even ordered to shave off their beards, the supreme humiliation.

Salvation from his brutal rule came in the form of England's King Richard the Lionheart, who docked at Limassol on his way to the Crusades. He crushed Comnenos and was welcomed by cheering crowds in Nicosia. After a few months, Richard left the island in the hands of Guy de Lusignan, a French former king of Jerusalem. Lusignan introduced barons from war torn Palestine with the promise of a safer life on Cyprus' fertile (and free) farm estates. The Lusignan dynasty's feudal rule reduced native Cypriots to serfdom. In 1260, the Roman Catholic Church was declared supreme on the island, though Orthodox priests maintained their status as the real spiritual authority inside the Greek-Cypriot community.

Genoese and Venetians

During the 14th century, Cyprus profited greatly as a Christian outpost, supplying the crusaders. Famagusta's merchants in particular became renowned for their extravagant wealth. The island's opulence attracted pirates, and fuelled a heated rivalry between the merchants of Genoa and Venice that erupted in bloody riots in 1345. The Cypriots sided with the Venetians against the Genoese, murdering merchants and looting shops in Famagusta. In retaliation, Genoa sent a fleet to ravage the island. In 1374, they extorted reparations of two million gold florins and confiscated the port of Famagusta.

By now, the Lusignan kings had become too weak to resist Italian demands. James II needed help from the Sultan of Egypt to oust the Genoese in 1464, but the gold it cost him emptied his treasury. By various intrigues, the Venetians stepped into the breach and ruled Cyprus for the next 82 years.

The Venetians' lucrative trade was threatened by Ottoman encroachment on three sides – Anatolia, the Levant and Egypt. In 1570, the Turks demanded that Venice give up Cyprus. Imagining that attack would come from the east, the Venetians consolidated their defences mainly in Famagusta. But the Turks landed on the south coast and took Nicosia in 46 days. The capital's Venetian commander was killed and his head sent as a warning to Marcantonio Bragadino, the commander at Famagusta. Undeterred, Bragadino led a heroic defence of the port city, with 8,000 Greek-Cypriot and Italian troops holding out for over 10 months against a Turkish army that was said to number 200,000. On 1 August 1571, with his ammunition gone, Bragadino surrendered. He was promised safe passage, but when the Turks saw they had lost

To defend their trade, the Venetians fortified Famagusta

Pafos Fort, used by the Turkish and the British

50,000 men to such a tiny army, they flayed Bragadino alive. Cyprus was now a province of the Ottoman Empire.

Turkish Rule

With the Turks controlling the whole of the eastern Mediterranean, Cyprus lost its strategic importance and was left to stagnate. The administrators proved more idle than oppressive and the island's infrastructure fell into ruin. The only advantage for the Greek Cypriots was the regained status of the Orthodox Church. By 1660, the Sultan made their archbishop directly responsible for the Cypriot citizenry.

During the Greek War of Independence of 1821, Archbishop Kyprianos let Greek rebel ships pick up supplies on the north coast. Turkey immediately sent 4,000 Syrian troops. The archbishop and three of his bishops were executed. More troops were brought from Egypt, resulting in large-scale massacres and the plunder of church property.

Over the next 50 years, the Sultan tried to halt widespread abuses by Turkish tax collectors, which were provoking massive emigration of both Greek and Turkish Cypriots. But local Turkish officials opposed all reforms, often resorting to armed intimidation of governors sent by the Sultan. The disintegration of Ottoman authority in Cyprus was symptomatic of the imminent collapse of the empire.

The British Step In

With 'the sick man of Europe' on his deathbed, the superpowers of the time hovered around like vultures to pick at the remains, among which Cyprus was a choice morsel. Britain was concerned that the eastern Mediterranean should remain safe for its ships to pass through the Suez Canal to India. To keep Russia out, Britain signed the Cyprus Convention with Turkey, whereby the island came under British administration while formally remaining the Sultan's possession. In 1878, the deal was sealed with a peaceful ceremony in Nicosia.

Greek Cypriots were happy about the transfer of power from corrupt Turks to upright Britons, and came to appreciate the new schools, hospitals, law courts and roads that had become the hallmarks of British colonial administration. The population rose from 186,000 in 1881 to 310,000 in 1921. But the most important contribution they expected from the British would be to help Cyprus achieve *enosis*, or union with Greece, as Britain had done for the Ionian Islands in 1864. As long as he was in opposition, Gladstone supported the claim, but he did nothing about it when he became prime minister.

Union with Greece was, of course, opposed by the Turkish-Cypriots. They remained calm, confident that Britain would respect its alliance with Turkey and not give in to demands for *enosis*. In 1914, Turkey sided with Germany in World War I and Britain promptly annexed Cyprus, claiming it as a British Crown Colony. More roads were built, but little was done to-

Statue of Archbishop
Makarios in Nicosia

wards *enosis*. In 1931, impatient Greek-Cypriot members of the Legislative Council resigned, and riots broke out in Nicosia. Troops were brought in from Egypt. Insurgent bishops were deported, political parties banned, the Greek flag outlawed and press censorship imposed. But during World War II, in response to the British alliance with Greece against Germany, Cypriots rallied to the British flag and furnished 30,000 troops. Political parties were duly reinstated.

The Fight for Unity

In 1945, Britain thought it was doing Cyprus a favour by moving it towards self-rule. But the Greek-Cypriot slogan of the day was '*enosis* and only *enosis*'. In 1950 a plebiscite of Greek Cypriots voted 96 percent in favour of union with Greece, and the Church appointed a new leader, Archbishop Makarios III *(see right)*.

In 1955, the campaign for *enosis* became an armed struggle, led by Lieutenant-Colonel George Grivas, a Cypriot-born Greek Army officer. Directed from a hideout deep in the Troodos Mountains, EOKA (the Greek initials for the National Organisation of Cypriot Fighters) conducted a campaign of bombing public buildings and assassinating opponents of *enosis*. Archbishop Makarios publicly disowned the actions, but gave EOKA clandestine support. He was exiled in 1956, first to the Seychelles and then to Athens.

In Greece itself the public gave noisy support to the Greek-Cypriot cause, but their government was reticent.

Turkey supported the Turkish-Cypriot opposition to *enosis* with two main arguments: the Muslim community would be defenceless if it was swallowed up in the greater Greek nation; and Greek extension to Cyprus would pose a military threat to Turkey. In 1958, Turkish Cypriots rioted in favour of partitioning the island.

In 1959, the Turkish and Greek Cypriots met in Zurich, agreeing to renounce both *enosis* and partition, while guaranteeing strict safeguards to protect the Turkish-Cypriot minority. The president of the new independent republic would be Greek-Cypriot Archbishop Makarios, and his vice-president would be the Turkish-Cypriot leader, Fazil Küçük. On 16 August 1960, Cyprus became independent, though still part of the British Commonwealth (with Britain retaining two military bases on the south coast). Grivas retired, unhappy, to Athens.

A Small Nation's Great Leader

In Archbishop Makarios, Cyprus was blessed with a first president of great intellect and spiritual authority. Born in 1913 to a peasant family in the Troodos Mountains, Mihail Christodoulous Mouskos became a monk at Kykkos Monastery. He studied in Athens and then Boston, before returning to Cyprus in 1948 to become Bishop of Kition (Larnaka).

Archbishop at the young age of 37, he won popular support with his dignified eloquence. But he was criticised by foreign observers for his failure to control Greek-Cypriot extremists, thus provoking alarm among Turkish Cypriots. Makarios, who died in 1977, impressed the world with his moral leadership of non-aligned nations at the height of the Cold War, and his courage during the Greek-inspired coup against him in 1974 and the subsequent Turkish invasion.

Troubled Independence

Kykkos Monastery, reputedly an EOKA base in the 1950s

Cabinet posts, parliamentary seats and civil service jobs were apportioned to Greek and Turkish Cypriots according to a fair ratio, and the main towns elected separate Greek- and Turkish-Cypriot municipal governments, but the constitution proved too complex to work. In 1963, Makarios proposed 13 simplifying amendments which the Turkish Cypriots vetoed, and fighting broke out in Nicosia. The British supervised a cease-fire and set up a 'Green Line' *(see right)* separating the communities. United Nations forces were brought in to patrol the Green Line in March 1964, and they have stayed ever since. Turkish-Cypriot enclaves were formed mainly in the northern part of the island, and Turkey and Greece each sent officers to train local forces.

In 1974, in a bid to gain popularity at home, Greece's military junta tried to impose *enosis* on Cyprus. Makarios resisted, demanding that the Greek officers withdraw. The junta responded by engineering a military attack on the Presidential Palace in Nicosia. Makarios escaped to Pafos and broadcast to the people of Cyprus, refuting reports of his assassination. This coup d'état gave Turkey a pretext to invade. Within three weeks, Turkish troops had occupied most of northern Cyprus. Makarios escaped to New York, where he rallied support in the UN to reinstate him as president. He died in 1977. The Turkish army remained in control of 37 percent of the island, including Famagusta, northern Nicosia and Keryneia. Some 170,000 Greek Cypriots were forced to flee to the south, while about 30,000 Turkish Cypriots migrated to the north. By 2005, approximately 80,000 settlers had been brought into Northern Cyprus from Turkey.

In 1983, the so-called Turkish Republic of Northern Cyprus was set up with Rauf Denktash as President, but it was recognised only by Turkey. The UN condemned the move and urged the leaders to find a way other than partition to protect minority rights on the island. Due to the diplomatic isolation of the Turkish north, the economy in the region stagnated. Greek Cypriots, on the other hand, recovered well from the shock of invasion; their economy thrived thanks mainly, but not exclusively, to tourism.

In 1998 the government of southern Cyprus entered into negotiations about possible entry into the European Union. The EU expressed a preference for Cyprus to join as a unit-

The Green Line

The Green Line, which marks the division between north and south Cyprus, owes its name to the British army officer who drew a line in green ink on a map to separate the warring Greek and Turkish Cypriot communities in Nicosia. Since the cease-fire in 1974, the line has extended across the entire island, and is formally known as the United Nations Buffer Zone. The line, which had been open for transit by non-Cypriot visitors from the South to the North under strictly controlled conditions, was opened in 2003 to freer movement in both directions, including by Cypriots. Since then the number of crossing points has increased and the terms of transit have been further relaxed.

ed country – a move that prompted various efforts towards peace and reunification. In April 2003 there was a shift in the stalemate over cross-border movement. In that month Denktash opened the Green Line *(see page 25)* and allowed citizens of both sides almost unconditional access.

Turkish-Cypriot elections in December 2003 paved the way for a further relaxing of the relationship. But additional UN talks held in early 2004 faltered just weeks ahead of the date set for the accession of Cyprus – at least the Greek-Cypriot South – to the EU. The UN's proposed agreement was put to referenda in both parts of the island. The Turkish Cypriots voted in favour and the Greek Cypriots against.

In 2004, the Republic of Cyprus joined the EU without Northern Cyprus. But momentum towards a settlement seemed to be growing. A new round of UN-sponsored consultations began in 2005. In March 2007, the Greek Cypriots unilaterally demolished their barricades at the Green Line on Odos Lidras (Ledra Street), which was Nicosia's main commercial artery before the capital was divided. The Turkish Cypriots promptly did the same on their side.

Tourism has enabled the Greek-Cypriot economy to thrive

In 2008, Demetris Christofias won the presidential election after promising to work towards unification. Shortly afterwards, peace talks between Christofias and Turkish Cypriot leader Mehmet Ali Talat began and the symbolic Odos Lidras Green Line crossing point was opened. The two leaders continue to meet, trying to establish the outlines of a possible settlement.

Historical Landmarks

c.10000BC First evidence of human occupation.

c.8200BC First permanent settlements on Cyprus.

c.3500BC Copper mines in Troodos foothills establish early wealth.

1200BC Mycenaean Greeks settle on the island.

700–350BC Invasions by Assyrians and Persians.

333BC Alexander the Great establishes Macedonian rule.

299BC Cyprus joins Hellenistic Egypt under the Ptolemy dynasty.

58BC Romans annexe Cyprus to their empire.

4th century AD Christianity takes hold; many churches built.

653 Arabs invade and install a garrison on the island.

965–1185 Middle Byzantine period. Cyprus flourishes.

1191–2 England's Richard the Lionheart defeats Isaac Comnenos and transfers the island to Guy de Lusignan, who founds a 300-year dynasty.

14th–15th centuries Cyprus grows rich from supplying crusaders but is pillaged by Genoese. Venetians take over from the Lusignans.

1571 Fall of Famagusta to the Turks ends Venetian rule.

1571–1878 Period of Turkish rule.

1878–1914 Cyprus under British administration, with Turkish possession. Turkey sides with Germany in 1914, so Britain annexes Cyprus.

1931 *Enosis* (unity with Greece) campaign builds force with riots.

1955 EOKA begins campaign of violence in pursuit of *enosis*.

1959–64 Turkish and Greek Cypriots form joint administration that leads to independence in 1960, but breaks down. UN intervenes.

1974 Coup by Greek military junta gives Turkey pretext to invade, occupying 37 percent of island.

1983 The 'Turkish Republic of Northern Cyprus' is declared by the North, but recognised only by Turkey.

2003 The Green Line in Nicosia is opened to relatively free movement between both sectors of the city.

2004 The Republic of Cyprus joins the EU without Northern Cyprus.

2007 Green Line barricades on Odos Lidras in Nicosia demolished.

2008 The euro is introduced in the South.

WHERE TO GO

If you really want to get to know Cyprus, rather than just soak up the sun on its beaches, you should plan to stay in more than one place. If your base is at one of South Cyprus' extremities – Pafos or Agia Napa – it's a good idea to spend a night or two at a more central coastal location, such as Limassol or Larnaka, or to go inland to Nicosia or the Troodos Mountains. With the North much more accessible than before, you may want to set aside time for this region.

> **Rapid transit**
>
> The motorway network linking Nicosia and the coastal resorts in South Cyprus makes for speedy transfers, but there's much to be said for pottering along on a slower route.

NICOSIA AND ENVIRONS

Nicosia (*Lefkosia* in Greek, *Lefkoşa* in Turkish) is Cyprus' only inland city. Situated on the site of ancient Ledra, today's city was founded in the 3rd century BC by Lefkos, son of Ptolemy I of Egypt. When the coastal towns of Pafos and Salamis came under Arab attack in the 7th century AD, the population shifted to the interior and Nicosia became the chief city. Under the Lusignans, it evolved into a splendid capital marked by elegant churches and monasteries in the French Gothic style.

Almost everything of interest to tourists is confined within, or just outside, the old city walls. The ramparts, hurriedly built by the Venetians in preparation for the Turkish invasion of 1570, remain Nicosia's dominant feature. The wheel-

Clear waters at Petra tou Romiou on the southwest coast

Sturdy Famagusta Gate

shaped Renaissance fortification has become the modern capital's distinctive logo, with its 11 pointed bastions and three giant gateways named after the three coastal cities to which they lead – Famagusta Gate to the east, Pafos Gate to the west and Keryneia (Girne) Gate to the north. Some of the bastions now shelter municipal offices, while sections of the (now dry) moat serve as public gardens, playgrounds and car parks.

When the Turkish invasion took place in 1974 the city was the scene of some of the heaviest fighting. Today Nicosia remains a divided city, half in Southern Cyprus, half in the North, and the UN buffer zone that runs along the dividing line, with its burnt-out, deserted buildings, UN checkpoints, barbed wire, sandbags and roadblocks, is an eerie reminder of this. However, the capital of Cyprus is undergoing something of a rebirth. Though UN peacekeepers still patrol the divided city's Green Line, since 2003 the line of division has been springing 'leaks'. Both tourists and Cypriots can now pass with relative ease between the two halves at a growing number of official crossing-points. Nicosians are starting to get to know each other again.

Many visitors spend just a day here, but an overnight stay is worthwhile if you want time to explore both halves of the fortified city properly. Be prepared for real heat – the city is around five degrees hotter than the coast, with temperatures soaring to 35°C (95°F) in summer.

Cyprus Archaeological Museum

The island's finest collection of antiquities is housed in the **Cyprus Archaeological Museum** (Archaiologiko Mouseio Kyprou; Tue–Fri 8am–4pm, Thur until 5pm, Sat 9am–4pm, Sun 10am–1pm; charge) on Leoforos Mouseiou, just west of the old walled city near the Pafos Gate. The neoclassical building houses archaeological artefacts dating from the Stone Age (around 10,000BC) to the time of the Roman Empire.

Exhibits from the Bronze Age include some of the first implements made from the island's copper mines, red-polished and white-painted pottery. Look out for the so-called sanctuary model (2000BC), in which worshippers and priests surround a bull sacrifice while a Peeping Tom on the sanctuary wall watches the secret ceremony. An intriguing Mycenaean *krater* (drinking cup) imported to Egkomi by merchants from the Peloponnese in the 14th century BC has an octopus motif framing a scene of Zeus preparing warriors for battle at Troy. Nearby, a beautiful blue faïence *rhyton* (ritual anointing vessel) from the 13th century BC depicts a lively bull-hunt in Kition. Fascinating royal tomb furniture from Salamis (8th century BC) includes an ivory throne, a bed, a sword and the remains of two chariots and their horses' skeletons.

Cyprus' Terracotta Army

Perhaps the most memorable highlight of the Cyprus Archaeological Museum is the 'Cyprus Terracotta Army', consisting of around 1,000 votive statues and figurines dating from between 625 and 500BC. Found at Agia Irini in northwest Cyprus, the figurines are displayed as they originally stood, around the altar of an open-air sanctuary. In a dual cult of war and fertility, soldiers, war chariots, priests with bull masks, sphinxes, Minotaurs and bulls were fashioned in all sizes, from life-size to just 10cm (4in) tall, according to their ritual importance.

Statue of *Aphrodite*

The monumental bronze of Emperor Septimius Severus (*c*.AD200) is a masterpiece of Roman-Cypriot art. In contrast, behind the imperious emperor is a movingly child-like *Sleeping Eros*. At the far end of the hall, a marble Aphrodite remains sensuous despite having lost her arms and lower legs.

A set of magnificent lions from the royal tombs at Tamassos *(see pages 39–40)* were discovered in 1997. Alongside them is a double-sided limestone stele depicting Bacchus on one side, and on the other, facing the wall, what is captioned an 'erotic scene'. Mildly erotic too is the famous *Leda and the Swan* mosaic taken from the Sanctuary of Aphrodite *(see page 75)*. Finally, look out for the gold pieces from the Lambousa Treasure Hoard and, in the last room, the small clay figures of women portrayed giving birth.

Outside the museum, you can cross the street to the shady **Municipal Gardens** (Dimotikos Kipos), home to the Cypriot parliament's House of Representatives and the **Lefkosia Municipal Theatre** (Dimotiko Theatro Lefkosias), the city's main venue for classical music, opera and dance. North of here on Leoforos Mouseiou is the Pafos Gate and a roundabout with a statue of EOKA fighter Markos Drakos throwing a grenade, and beyond up Leoforos Markou Drakou is the **Ledra Palace Hotel** Green Line crossing-point *(see page 79)*.

Around Odos Lidras

Today, most visitors to the old city enter through **Plateia Eleftherias**, a prominent square just south of the walled city that is home to the Town Hall. The old city's principal thoroughfare and main pedestrianised shopping street, **Odos Lidras** (Ledra Street), runs north of here to the Green Line.

Just off the southern end of the street, at 17 Odos Ippokratous, is the award-winning **Leventis Municipal Museum of Nicosia** (Dimotiko Mouseio Leventi Lefkosias; Tue–Sun 10am–4.30pm; free but donation appreciated), which presents a beautifully designed account of Nicosia's history. Displayed in a fine 19th-century neoclassical mansion, the exhibits include costumes, utensils, coins and ceramics.

Just behind the museum is the revived **Laiki Geitonia** (Popular Neighbourhood), which purports to recreate the atmosphere of old Nicosia. Various buildings in traditional style, some restored, others specially constructed, house quaint shops and tavernas, plus artisans' galleries where you can watch the craftsmen at work. Though it is a slightly contrived tourist enclave, it is a popular spot that is particularly pretty at night.

Slightly further up Odos Lidras, the **Ledra Museum-Observatory** (Ledra Mouseio-Paratereterio; daily 10am–8pm; charge) on the top floor of the Debenhams department store, gives excellent views of the whole city, including the walls and Green Line. The northern end of Odos Lidras passes through the **buffer zone**. Heavy barricades, erected here in 1964 after a flare up of ethnic violence, were removed in April 2008 and the street is

Tourist office

There is an office of the Cyprus Tourism Organisation in Laiki Geitonia (at 11 Odos Aristokyprou), from which free walking tours of the city depart on Monday, Thursday, and Friday at 10am.

Omeriye Mosque's minaret

now the site of a popular crossing point between the two halves of the city.

East of Odos Lidras along Odos Nikokleous is the landmark church of **Panagia Faneromeni** (Birth of the Virgin; open irregularly; free). Although it only dates from 1872–3 in its present form, it is a mix of several styles and features a fine iconostasis. Alongside the church is a small, squat, old mosque, which is usually closed to the public.

Around the Archbishop's Palace

It is worth strolling around the neighbourhood in the eastern half of Old Nicosia to see the effects of one of the restoration projects that has been transforming parts of the city. Formerly crumbling, the walls of the fine Ottoman-era mansions and townhouses have been shored up and painted in a variety of colours, and their interiors renovated.

Southeast of Panagia Faneromeni is **Omeriye Mosque** (Omeriye Camii) with its landmark minaret, which was transformed from the Augustinian monastery church of St Mary's by the city's 16th-century Turkish conquerors. The mosque is still used by Muslim worshippers and is open to visitors (don't forget to remove your shoes).

Just east of the mosque on Odos Patriarchou Grigoriou is the **House of Hadjigeorgakis Kornesios** (Archontiko Hatsigeorgakis Kornesiou; Tue–Fri 8.30am–3.30pm, Thur until 5pm, Sat 9.30am–3.30pm; charge), also known as the

Konak Mansion, a beautiful 18th-century structure with a Gothic-style doorway and overhanging, enclosed balcony. The Ottoman-style interior is notable for its period furniture and carpets, ornate stairway and grand reception room. It testifies to the wealth of Kornesios, the *dragoman*, or official mediator between the Turkish sultan and Cypriot archbishop.

North of here on Plateia Archiepiskopou Kyprianou, the **Archbishop's Palace** (Archiepiskopiko Megaro) is a curious modern pastiche of Venetian architecture. Amid the splendour of the state rooms (occasionally open for tours), Archbishop Makarios III installed an austere bedroom with a simple iron bed.

Housed in the public wing of the palace is one of the island's finest museums, the **Byzantine Museum and Art Galleries** (Byzantino Mouseio kai Pinakothikes; Mon–Fri 9am–4.30pm, Sat 9am–1pm; charge). This institution has

Inside the House of Hadjigeorgakis Kornesios

rescued and restored a superb collection of icons from all over Cyprus. Presented with loving care, it offers the island's full range of Byzantine art, from a primitive 9th-century Virgin Mary to some examples that demonstrate the genre's decline in the 18th century. Don't miss the display of 33 splendid 6th-century mosaics from Panagia Kanakaria church in Northern Cyprus, which were recovered through court action in the 1990s, after having been looted and offered for sale on the international art market.

An icon of Christ on display at the Byzantine Museum

Next to the museum is **Agios Ioannis** (St John's; Mon–Fri 8am–noon and 2–4pm, Sat 8am–noon; free), Nicosia's small Orthodox cathedral, built in 1665 in an approximation of Late Gothic style. Its colourful 18th-century frescoes, which cover the walls and ceiling, depict landmarks in the island's early Christian history.

The adjacent Gothic-arcaded monastery building, which was the Archbishop's Palace before the present one was built, is now the **Ethnographic Museum of Cyprus** (Ethnografiko Mouseio Kyprou; Mon–Fri 9am–4pm; charge) and displays wooden water wheels, looms, pottery, carved and painted bridal chests, lace, embroidered costumes and much else besides.

Next door is the **National Struggle Museum** (Mouseio Agonos; July–Aug Mon–Fri 8am–2pm, Sept–June Mon–Fri 8am–2pm, Thur also 3–5.30pm; charge). The museum documents the EOKA armed uprising against British rule in the 1950s. On display are weapons, old newspapers and a small, red Hillman that was the command car of EOKA leader Griva Digenis. Opposite is the Pancyprian Gymnasium, a school famous for its *enosis* activism in the 1950s.

In the Podocataro bastion of the city wall near here, the marble-and-bronze **Liberty Monument** (Mnimeio tis Eleftherias) recalls EOKA's war of liberation to free Cyprus from British rule. Slightly further north around the battlements is the massive tunnel-like **Famagusta Gate** (Pyli Ammochostou; May–Sept Mon–Fri 10am–1pm and 5–8pm, Oct–Apr Mon–Fri 10am–1pm and 4–7pm; free), which was originally the main entrance to the old city. It has been restored and is used as a cultural centre. The stone barrel vaults provide an atmospheric setting for concerts, plays and modern art exhibitions.

Between Famagusta Gate and the Green Line is another restored Ottoman-era neighbourhood. Centred on the church of **Panagia Chrysaliniotissa** (Our Lady of the Golden Flax; open when the priest is around; free but donation appreciated), this tranquil area has perhaps even more characteristic period architecture than around the Archbishop's Palace.

Northern Nicosia

Compared with the thriving southern half of the city, northern Nicosia is quieter and poorer but, as with much of the North, this is changing fast. The crossing point on Odos Lidra (Ledra Street) is conveniently close to a cluster of the most interesting sights in the North, making even the shortest of visits worthwhile.

To the east of the Odos Lidra crossing point you will see the minarets and lofty Gothic arches of the **Selimiye Camii**

(Selimiye Mosque; daily dawn–dusk; donation expected), which was formerly the great Cathedral of the Holy Wisdom, begun in 1209 and completed in the 14th century. The Lusignans were crowned kings of Cyprus and Christians worshipped here until the Turks turned it into a mosque after the 1570 conquest.

Next door is the **Bedesten** (covered market), which dates from the 12th to the 14th century, when it was built as the church of St Nicholas-of-the-English. The Turks converted it into a market – today disused. You can still admire the Gothic doors and religious sculptures, the barrel-shaped roof and the dome. The building is currently undergoing extensive renovations. Across the street is a functioning bazaar, the **Belediye Pazari** (Municipal Market), or Bandabulya. Behind the mosque is the **Sultan Arşivine** (Sultan's Library; daily, summer 9am–2pm, winter 9am–1pm and 2–4.45pm; charge) housing rare books in Turkish, Arabic and Persian.

West of the mosque, Asma Alti Sokağı leads northwest past a couple of old Turkish *hans* (inns) with picturesque courtyards and verandahs: the **Büyük Han** (Great Inn), now home to small art galleries, workshops, handicraft shops and a restaurant, and used as a venue for cultural activities, and the **Kumarcı-**

Selimiye Mosque

lar Hanı (Gamblers' Inn), which now houses the Northern Cyprus Antiquities and Culture Office. Built by the Turks in the 18th century as hospices for visiting foreigners, the two inns are rare survivors of their kind on the island. Also in this area is the **Büyük Hamam** (Great Bath), a modernised Turkish bath house. At the far end of Asma Alti Sokağı is **Atatürk Meydanı**, the square that is

Venetian coat of arms on Atatürk Meydanı

the hub of Turkish-Cypriot Nicosia. At its centre is a granite column probably brought from Salamis by the Venetians.

From the square, head north along Girne Caddesi to the **Mevlevi Tekke** (daily, summer 9am–2pm, winter 9am–1pm and 2–4.45pm; charge). This was once a ceremonial hall used by the Mevlevi 'whirling dervish' sect, outlawed in Turkey in 1925. The multi-domed, 17th-century building now has a small Turkish ethnographical collection with a reconstruction of the whirling dervishes' dance floor complete with mannequins. The building itself is the star exhibit, but an arresting sight is the room packed with the tombs of 16 Mevlevi sheiks. Beyond here, the **Keryneia Gate** (Girne Kapısı) is northern Nicosia's only original Venetian gate, leading to the rest of Northern Cyprus (see pages 79–85).

Around Nicosia

The following excursions are all within 50km (30 miles) of Nicosia, making them easy day trips.

The site of **Tamassos**, an ancient city-kingdom built on copper mining, is just over 20km (12 miles) southwest of the capital, near the village of Politiko. Here excavations have uncovered a sanctuary and altar dedicated to Aphrodite, although the importance of the find is difficult for the lay person to appreciate (it seems to be nothing but knee-high rubble). Of more general interest are the two royal tombs (6th century BC). In each, stairways descend to a narrow *dromos* – a passage carved in stone to imitate wooden dwellings, complete with simulated bolted doors, window sills and 'log-roof' ceilings. A set of magnificent stone lions and sphinxes from the site are on display at the Cyprus Archaeological Museum *(see page 32)*.

Nearby is the monastery of **Agios Irakleidios** (Sun–Fri 9am–5pm), which is now in the hands of nuns who tend its gardens. After many restorations, the present 18th-century church houses, in a domed mausoleum, the remains of the saint who guided Paul and Barnabas on their mission to Cyprus. Hera-

At work in the fields around Tamassos

kleidios, the first bishop of Tamassos, was burned alive by unbelievers; his skull and a bone from his hand were salvaged and are treasured in a bejewelled gold reliquary.

From here it is a short journey to the monastery of **Machairas**, 884m (2,900ft) up in the rugged Pitsilia region (groups only Mon, Tue and Thur 9am–noon; free but donation appreciated). But once you are there, the

Mosaic above a door at Machairas Monastery

views make it all worthwhile. The monastery itself is a modern construction; an 1892 fire destroyed the original 12th-century foundation, although an allegedly miracle-working icon of the Virgin Mary has survived.

The region was a natural hideout for the EOKA second-in-command Grigoris Afxentiou, who died in a battle with the British near the monastery in 1957. The site of his death (a cave just below the monastery) is decorated with wreaths and is a place of pilgrimage for Greek Cypriots.

Down the road beyond Gourri, the village of **Fikardou** represents a worthy effort to sustain Cypriot rural traditions. The whole village is protected as an Ancient Monument and a Unesco World Heritage Site. Its subtly coloured 18th- and 19th-century ironstone houses and cobbled streets have been restored. The idea was not to create a folk museum, but to revitalise the community. Alas, it does not seem to be working. In 1992, when the scheme was in its infancy, there were just eight permanent residents. It was hoped that others might be enticed by the handsome reconstruction, but the population has remained at about the same number ever since.

Asinou Church's plain exterior belies the dazzling art within

Wind your way past the church and the crumbling old buildings to the museum houses of **Katsinioros** and **Achilleas Dimitri** (June–Aug Tue–Fri 9.30am–4.30pm, Sat 9.30am–4pm, Sun 10am–1.30pm, Sept–May Tue–Fri 9am–4pm, Sat 9am–3.30pm, Sun 10.30am–2pm; charge), where you can see authentic old furnishings, a spinning wheel and loom, a wine press and a brandy still.

Asinou Church

Stranded somewhat in the middle of nowhere, at Asinou, just outside Nikitari, 50km (31 miles) west of Nicosia, is **Panagia tis Asinou** (Our Lady of Asinou), also known as Panagia tis Forviotissas (Our Lady of the Meadows; daily 9.30am–5pm, Sept–Oct until 4.30pm, Nov–Apr until 4pm; free but donation appreciated), also known as Panagia Forviotissa, one of the gems of the Troodos foothills. From Nicosia take the road beyond Peristerona, then follow the signs to the 12th-century hillside church, which is famous for its magnificent Byzantine frescoes (see also page 65).

This modest but exquisite little church of ochre stone contains a veritable gallery of Byzantine art from the 12th to 16th century. A booklet explaining the different styles and subjects of the frescoes is usually available. But for a scene that is sublime beyond art, look back through the narthex to the frescoes framing the west door, open to the green wooded slope beyond. If you find the church closed go back to the village of Nikitari and search out the local priest who looks after the key.

LARNAKA AND THE EAST

Embedded on the western shore of the wide bay that bears its name, bustling **Larnaka** retains a holiday resort atmosphere whilst playing an important role in the Cypriot economy. It has Cyprus' main international airport, the country's second busiest port (after Limassol) and is an important industrial base.

Much of northern Larnaka is built over the ancient city-kingdom of Kition. Legend attributes its founding to Kittim, a grandson of Noah, and excavated dwellings from the 2nd millennium BC make this the oldest continuously inhabited city in Cyprus. Phoenicians prospered here from the export of copper, and many centuries later Lusignan barons revived the town as a commercial and shipping centre. Under the Turks, foreign merchants and the consulates needed to protect their interests gave the town a cosmopolitan air.

Larnaka's Agios Lazaros

The Seafront

The palm-lined **Foinikoudes** (Palm Trees) **Promenade** is home to hotels, international restaurants, chic cafés and fast-food eateries. At the north end is the pleasure-boat marina. A bust of the Athenian commander Kimon, who led a fleet to recapture Kition from the Persians in 450BC (but died in the attempt), is a reminder of an ancient past.

From the marina, the dark, compacted, sandy town beach stretches almost to the old fort that marks the heart of what was the Turkish quarter. **Larnaka Fort** (Frourio Larnakas; Mon–Fri, June–Aug 9am–7.30pm, Sept–May 9am–5pm; charge), built by the Turks in 1625, houses exhibits from its own history and serves as a venue for cultural events. From the ramparts, there are good views of the harbour. Opposite is the **Cami Kebir** (Great Mosque; dawn–dusk; donation expected), founded in the late 16th century and still functioning as a place of worship. Notice the tombstones topped with stone turbans in the graveyard, a rare sight so close to a mosque.

Turbanned tombstones in the Cami Kebir's graveyard

Agios Lazaros

Inland from here, at the end of Odos Dionysou, is the three-tiered campanile of the town's most revered church, **Agios Lazaros** (St Lazarus'; daily, Apr–Aug 8am–12.30pm and 3.30–6.30pm, Sept–Mar 8am–12.30pm and 2.30–5pm; free but donation appreciated), dedicated to the man the New Testament tells us Jesus raised from the dead. According to legend, the locals of Bethany, his home town, were not much impressed by the miracle, and Lazarus was expelled in a not particularly seaworthy boat that nevertheless got him as far as Kition. Here, where he was more appreciated, Lazarus settled, became bishop and died (this time for good). The church erected over his tomb has been rebuilt many times. Its present style is a mix of extravagant Byzantine, Romanesque and Gothic styles, and it has a fine iconostasis. The purported remains of Lazarus were removed from here in 890 and taken to Constantinople. In the crypt below the iconostasis you can see the empty but still venerated sarcophagus.

Larnaka's Museums

Opposite the marina, housed in refurbished former customs warehouses, are the **Larnaka Town Museum** (Mouseio tis Polis tis Larnakas) and **Tornaritis-Pierides Palaeontology Museum** (Palaiontologiko Mouseio Pieridis-Tornaritis; both Tue–Fri 9am–2pm, Sat–Sun 9am–noon, closed Sun June–Aug; free). The former has displays of coins, art, folk art and more; and the latter has exhibits covering some 500 million years of the island's natural history, including some on extinct indigenous species like the pygmy hippopotamus and pygmy elephant. Just inland is the **tourist office**, from where walking tours of Larnaka depart twice a week.

Across from the tourist office, on Odos Zinonos Kitieos, is the town's finest historical collection, the **Pierides Foundation Archaeological Museum** (Archaiologiko Mouseio tou Idrymatos Pieridi; Mon–Thur 9am–4pm, Fri–Sat 9am–1pm; charge). Housed in an old family mansion are hundreds of archaeological finds and works of art, tracing Cypriot history from neolithic to late-Byzantine times. Highlights include pots made of carved stone and red-polished clay, idols of Astarte (the Phoenician counterpart to, or forerunner of, Aphrodite), medieval glazed ceramics, Roman glassware and Cypriot embroidery, costumes and furniture. Situated next to the museum is a sculpture garden containing several avant-garde pieces.

Larnaka District Archaeological Museum (Archaiologiko Mouseio Eparchias Larnakas; Tue–Fri 8am–3pm, Thur until

Hala Sultan Tekke, the island's most important Muslim shrine

5pm, Sat 9am–3pm; charge) is a 10-minute walk northwest of the city centre, at the corner of Odos Kilkis and Odos Kimonos. Of principal interest here are the prehistoric finds from the nearby sites of Choirokoitia (*see page 49*), Kalavasos and Kition. Uphill, just beyond the museum, the paltry remains of the **Kition Acropolis** (Akropolis tou Kitiou), dating back to the 13th century BC, will probably appeal only to archaeology buffs.

West of Larnaka

About 3km (2 miles) southwest of the town, in the direction of the airport, lies the Salt Lake that provided a valuable source of income to ancient Larnaka. Lying 3m (10ft) below sea level, it is a true lake only in spring. The salt was once collected each year at the end of July, after the lake dried up, but today pollution has rendered it unfit for human consumption. In autumn and winter migratory flamingos feed here, although their numbers have declined in recent years.

➎ The **Hala Sultan Tekke** (daily, June–Aug 7.30am–7.30pm, Apr–May and Sept–Oct 9am–6pm, Nov–Mar 9am–5pm; free but donation appreciated), a Muslim shrine, looks like a mirage in the dry summer, thrusting its minaret through greenery and palm trees above the blinding salt flats. The shrine contains the remains of the Prophet Mohammed's wet nurse, Umm Haram ('Sacred Mother'), known as Hala Sultan in Turkish, and is Cyprus' most important place of Muslim pilgrimage. According to tradition, Umm Haram came to Cyprus with Arab invaders in 649. She fell from her mule near the Salt Lake, broke her neck and was buried here. The Turks built the mosque around the shrine in 1816.

The outer room has brightly painted octagonal columns and there is a gallery for women to the right. In the inner sanctuary, the guardian (who also acts as a guide) will point out the trilithon structure above Umm Haram's grave – two enormous stones about 4.5m (15ft) high, covered with a meteorite said to have come from Mt Sinai and to have hovered in the air here by itself for centuries.

Some 8km (5 miles) further is the village of Kiti and its church of **Panagia Angeloktisti** (Our Lady 'Built by Angels'; daily, June–Aug 8am–noon and 2–6pm, Sept–May 8am–noon and 2–4pm; free but donation appreciated). Constructed in honey-toned stone, the domed 11th-century edifice replaces a much earlier structure. Its outstanding feature is a splendid early Byzantine **mosaic** in the apse, which is among the finest works of Byzantine art in Cyprus. The standing Virgin Mary holds the Christ Child, flanked by the archangels Michael and Gabriel.

While you're in this area, you should continue through Perivolia to the coast at **Cape Kiti** (Akrotirio Kiti). Here, tourism developments have burgeoned on what was once a lonely, remote spot, which had not much more than a lighthouse and a medieval watch tower to mark the scenic cape.

Red Villages

The southeast corner of Cyprus is not only a major resort area, but the island's vegetable garden. Potatoes, aubergines, tomatoes, cucumbers and onions are all grown for export in the fertile red soil of the Kokkinochoria (Red Villages) district.

Stavrovouni, Lefkara and Choirokoitia

The famous mountain-top monastery of **Stavrovouni** (Mountain of the Cross; daily, Apr–Aug 8am–noon and 3–6pm, Sept–Mar 8am–noon and 2–5pm; free but donation appreciated; men only) is located west of Larnaca, just off the A1 road to Nicosia. At an altitude of 689m (2,260ft), it has superb views north to Nicosia and the hazy Pentadaktylos Mountains, and south over terraced hills to the Salt Lake, Larnaka and the sea.

The church at the mountain-top monastery of Stavrovouni

Stavrovouni was built on the site of a shrine to Aphrodite which, like the monastery today, was off-limits to women. Nevertheless, Helena, mother of Emperor Constantine, is said to have ventured up here in AD330 to found the monastery and endow it with a piece of the True Cross. The relic is still proudly displayed in the monastery church. Note that cameras are forbidden anywhere in the grounds.

At the foot of the winding road up to Stavrovouni is the monastery of **Agia Varvara** (St Barbara), open in the morning and late afternoon (closed noon–3pm). Over the road is the studio of Brother Kallinikos. He is world-renowned as one of the best contemporary icon painters in the Orthodox Church. It is fascinating to watch the elderly monk at work in his chaotic studio, where some of his icons are for sale.

Lefkara, 40km (25 miles) west of Larnaka, is actually two villages, Pano Lefkara and Kato Lefkara, on a picturesque site in the foothills of the Troodos Mountains. Lefkara is synonymous with *lefkaritika*, the traditional embroidery that has brought the village fame for more than five centuries. Widely but incorrectly termed 'lacework', *lefkaritika* is actually linen openwork, stitched with intricate geometric patterns.

Women still work in the narrow streets and courtyards of Pano (Upper) Lefkara, patiently turning out embroidered articles which you can buy from them or in one of the many shops. A few years ago there were fewer than a dozen outlets; today there are more than 50. As a result, hustling, albeit of a mild kind, is common practice.

Smaller and mostly overlooked by the tour groups is Kato (Lower) Lefkara. It is an attractive village, with many of its traditional houses recently restored and window and door frames painted in bright Mediterranean blue.

Archaeologically inclined visitors should head south to Choirokoitia, a village that is home to the **Choirokoitia** **Neolithic Settlement** (Archaiologikos Choros Choirokoitias; daily, Apr–May and Sept–Oct 8am–6pm, June–Aug 8am–7.30pm, Nov–Mar 8am–5pm; charge). One of the oldest sites in Cyprus, it dates back to 7000BC. The most interesting of the four areas is the main street with its foundations of beehive-shaped houses called *tholoi*. Artefacts discovered here are on show at Nicosia's Cyprus Archaeological Museum (*see page 31*).

Lefkara is famous for intricate *lefkaritika* embroidery

East to Agia Napa

Just beyond the resort hotels east of Larnaka, you pass through the **Dhekelia British Sovereign Base Area**. Here the Greek-Cypriot territory is squeezed into a narrow strip along the border of the Turkish-occupied zone. East of Dhekelia is **Potamos**, a picturesque creek that's invariably jammed with small, gaily painted fishing boats, flanked by a couple of authentic seafood tavernas.

In the years following the Turkish occupation of Famagusta, **Agia Napa** was transformed from a tiny fishing village into Cyprus' major resort. Indeed, in recent years it has become one of the Mediterranean's best-known dance-club destinations *(see page 93)*. As you enter the town, its character is evident from the international bars, restaurants and seaside souvenir shops, but the change is most pronounced in the square around the monastery of **Agia Napa** (Our Lady of the Forest; daily dawn–dusk; free). Today, apart from a sycamore said to be 600 years old, the only forest is that of the concrete pillars and neon signs that mark the island's largest concentration of bars and nightclubs.

However, during the day (when the clubbers are asleep or at the beach), the square and monastery are often peaceful. The monastery, built around 1530, remains one of

On the beach at Agia Napa

Cyprus' most handsome Venetian buildings, with an octagonal marble fountain in the Gothic cloister. It is now a conference centre for the World Council of Churches, and its church is only open regularly for Sunday services.

Another cultural attraction of note is the **Thalassa Sea Museum** (Thalassio Mouseio 'Thalassa'; May Mon 9am–1pm, Tue–Sat 9am–5pm, June–Sept Mon 9am–1pm, Tue–Sat 9am–1pm and 6pm–10pm; charge), next door to the tourist office. It contains shells, fossils and taxidermic marine specimens and a replica of the ancient Kyrenia ship *(see page 81)*.

Varosha boat trip

An intriguing boat trip from Agia Napa goes past the Green Line as far as Famagusta to view the decaying town of Varosha. Once a major resort, it has been left to rot since 1974, when it was declared UN territory (though it is policed by the Turkish army). Now that travel to the North has been eased, you can also drive around Varosha's outskirts on the Famagusta side, but you still can't enter or take pictures.

Agia Napa's growth is largely a result of its fine beaches of golden sand. The main one is **Nissi Beach**, a picture-postcard strip and cove with limpid blue waters and a tiny island within paddling distance. At nearby **Makronisos**, another popular beach, there are 19 rock tombs dating from the classical and Hellenistic periods.

Cape Gkreko

For anyone who can't quite see the point of staying up all night in the clubs of Agia Napa, there's **Cape Gkreko** (Akrotirio Gkreko), the island's southeastern tip, where spectacular rocky inlets, caves and bays provide an escape from the crowds.

Head east on the coast road towards the cape and just outside Agia Napa, beside the Grecian Bay Hotel, you'll find the

A view of the coast near Cape Gkreko

Thalassines Spilies (Sea Caves), which are famous for a much-photographed sea arch and frequented by snorkellers and divers. A few kilometres further along the main road are the more spectacular **Spilies sta Palatia** (Palace Caves).

Further still is the **Cape Gkreko viewpoint**. You will have to walk the last 500m (1,600ft) uphill, but it is well worth the effort. From an altitude of almost 100m (330ft), the clifftop view looking west is stupendous. Just to the east is Cape Gkreko itself. The point is occupied by transmitters belonging to Radio Monaco International and is off-limits.

Heading north will bring you to **Konnos Bay**, one of the most picturesque sandy coves in Cyprus. On a quiet day, it can be heaven. In midsummer, Agia Napa 'booze cruises' (or 'orgy boats') and their sound systems disturb the peace.

The coast road continues north to the lovely sandy beaches of Fig Tree Bay, around which the purpose-built resort of **Protaras** has sprung up.

LIMASSOL AND THE SOUTH COAST

Limassol (*Lemesos* in Greek) is Cyprus' good-time town, with many restaurants and a brash and boisterous nightlife. Fittingly, it plays host to the island's most exuberant pre-Lenten Carnival. In addition, it boasts Cyprus' busiest harbour and is the focal-point of much of the wine industry. Most accommodation is away from the centre in a strip of high-rise hotels 5–10km (3–6 miles) east.

It was at Limassol that the crusading English king Richard the Lionheart stopped off in 1191. He defeated the tyrannical Byzantine usurper Isaac Comnenos, then proceeded to sell off Cyprus – first to the Knights Templar (who settled in Limassol), and then to the Lusignans *(see page 18)*. The crusader Knights of St John made Limassol their headquarters in 1291, when the town flourished as never before.

By the early 19th century, earthquakes and the rapacity of the Genoese and Turks had reduced the city to a crumbling village. British development of the wine industry breathed new life into it and, since the 1974 partition, Limassol's population has almost doubled, to 190,000, second only to that of Nicosia.

The only surviving monument to the town's feudal glory is **Limassol Castle** (Kastro tis Lemesou), an imposing, 13th-century stone fortification near the old port. Today it houses the **Cyprus Medieval Museum** (Mesaioniko Mouseio tis Kyprou; Tue–Sat 9am–5pm, Sun 10am–1pm; charge), the

Modern sculpture on display at Limassol's seafont

View of Limassol's rooftops from the castle battlements

island's best collection from this period, with some well-preserved tombstones, and suits of armour that reflect the local metalworking tradition. The building itself is also interesting and has fine views from the battlements.

The area around the castle is particularly pleasant, with tropical gardens and a clutch of attractive pavement cafés and historic buildings. The narrow lanes around here used be the Turkish commercial quarter. You can enter the **Cami Kebir** (Great Mosque), which lies a few metres from the castle and is still in use. Behind it, you can peer into the remnants of an older mosque. There's a working Turkish bath *(hamam)* nearby. Also in this interesting quarter, you will find artisans' workshops where the speciality is metalware (particularly copper and tin), plus a carob mill and warehouse dating from the early 1900s, which have been restored and transformed into a cultural and shopping centre with restaurants and cafés.

From the mosque, it's a 10-minute walk along Odos Agiou Andreou to the **Municipal Folk Art Museum** (Dimotiko Mouseio Laikis Technis; Mon–Fri, Thur am only, June–Sept 8.30am–1.30pm and 4–6.30pm, Oct–May 8.30am–1.30pm and 3–5.30pm; charge). It provides a glimpse of rural Cypriot life through wood-carving, embroidery and weaving.

Further east, adjacent to the the seafront promenade, are the **Municipal Gardens** (Dimotikos Kipos), a pleasant place to rest for a while. There's also a miniature 'zoo' here that contains mostly birds. At the far end of the gardens, the small, modern **Lemesos District Archaeological Museum** (Archaiologiko Mouseio Eparchias Lemesou; Tue–Fri 8am–3pm, Thur until 5pm, Sat 9am–3pm; charge) contains fascinating archaeological treasures, among them jewellery and expressive terracotta figurines. There's a head of Aphrodite from Kourion and a massive statue of the Egyptian god Bes from ancient Amathous *(see below)*.

Wine-making in Cyprus is not only an industry but also a tourist attraction. The top **wineries** *(oinopoleia)*, KEO, ETKO and SODAP, cluster together on Leoforos Fragklinou Rousvelt, west of the castle. All offer short tours which usually begin at 9.30 or 10am and end with a tasting.

East of the town, hidden among the beach resort hotels, are the ruins of ancient **Amathous** (daily, June–Aug 8am–7.30pm, Apr–May and Sept–Oct 8am–6pm, Nov–Mar 8am–5pm;

Stone carvings in the Folk Art Museum

charge), one of the island's oldest city-kingdoms. The remains are centred on the city's monumental *agora* (marketplace), and include basilicas, a temple of Aphrodite and an aqueduct.

A few kilometres further on is **Governor's Beach** (Paralia Akti Kyberniti), a dark-sand beach with various hotel and villa developments. A local bus connects it with Limassol. Farther east along the coast road, you come to **Zygi**, a seafront village with an old jetty and a cluster of fish restaurants that are popular with Cypriot seafood aficionados.

West of Limassol

Traces of one of the earliest phases of human presence on the island – hunters of pygmy hippos from 9000BC – were found on the **Akrotiri Peninsula** west of Limassol. Half of the peninsula is made up of salt lake – more flats than lake – popular with migratory birds, notably pink flamingos, from October to March. Most of the remainder of the peninsula is occupied by the airfield and other installations of the British Akrotiri/Episkopi Sovereign Base Area.

Just south of Akrotiri village, a bumpy track leads east to **Agios Nikolaos ton Gaton** (St Nicholas of the Cats; daily; free). The fame of the monastery has everything to do with the snake-hunting cats its monks reared; today's institution is a modern building with little of historical or architectural interest, but a considerable degree of flower-bedecked charm, run by a handful of nuns.

13 North of the peninsula, the impressive 15th-century **Kolossi Castle** (Kastro tou Kolossiou; daily, June–Aug 8am–7.30pm, Apr–May and Sept–Oct 8am–6pm, Nov–Mar 8am–5pm; charge) is one of the icons of Cypriot tourism. Once the headquarters of the Knights of St John, from here they administered their considerable sugar plantations and vineyards. The *Commanderie*, as the headquarters was known, gave its name to their prized Commandaria dessert wine, still produced today.

Among the rooms, all now empty, the one with a huge fireplace was the kitchen. In the adjacent room is a damaged fresco, the only surviving decoration. Climb the steep, narrow spiral staircase for the view from the battlements. Outside you can see traces of an ancient aqueduct and an imposing Gothic structure that served as a sugar refinery.

Kourion

Before exploring the great archaeological site of Kourion, stop in the nearby village of Episkopi to do a little homework at the **Kourion Archaeological Museum** (Archaiologiko Mouseio Kourio; Mon–Fri 9am–2.30pm, Sept–July also Thur 3–5pm; charge), which holds dramatic finds from the earthquake that devastated Kourion in AD365. On display is a touching group of three human skeletons: archaeologists believe them to be of a 25-year-old male protecting a 19-year-old female

Kourion's Roman theatre

The House of the Gladiators

with an 18-month-old baby clutched to her breast. Other exhibits include a Roman stone lion fountain, terracotta vases and figurines.

Just west of Episkopi is **Kourion** itself (daily, June–Aug 8am–7.30pm, Apr–May and Sept–Oct 8am–6pm, Nov–Mar 8am–5pm; charge). Along with Salamis in the north (see page 85), it is the island's most important archaeological site. Not the least of its attractions is its spectacular setting high on a bluff above Episkopi Bay. In ancient times, sacrilegious criminals were hurled to their death on to the rocks below.

Experts attribute the foundation of the town to Mycenaean settlers in the 13th century BC. Known as Curium to the Romans, it converted to Christianity in the 4th century, with its faith sorely tested by a devastating earthquake in 365. After Arab raids in the 7th century, the bishopric moved out to what is now Episkopi, leaving Kourion to sink into oblivion.

The site is large. Your first stop is the reconstructed **Roman theatre** (AD50–175), occupying a spectacular site on the edge of the bluff. The theatre once seated 3,500 and is now used for open-air performances. Behind the theatre is the Roman **Villa of Eustolios**. The floor mosaics of birds and fish indicate that Eustolios was a man of wealth and taste; inscriptions to both Apollo and Christ suggest that, at least from a religious perspective, he was prudent enough to hedge his bets. Eustolios later added a bathhouse, which he opened to destitute survivors of the earthquake, as attested by an inscription.

The central room features some more remarkable mosaics, including one of Ktisis, a deity who personifies creation.

The extensive ruins of the city include the *agora* (marketplace) and *nymphaeum* (fountain house). Unfortunately, this area is likely to be inaccessible as excavations continue. Turn to the left to explore the remains of an early Christian **basilica**. The basilica's plan reveals 12 pairs of granite columns for the nave. To the north is the baptistry, where congregants disrobed and were anointed with oil before descending to the font.

Opposite are the ruins of a colonnaded portico paved with the so-called **Achilles mosaic**. It depicts Achilles, disguised as a woman to avoid enlistment in the expedition to Troy, being tricked by Odysseus into grabbing a spear and shield and revealing his identity. The nearby **House of the Gladiators** is so named for its mosaics of two duels, one with an aristocratic-looking referee – perhaps the owner of the house.

The remains of a public bathhouse

The Sanctuary of Apollo Ylatis

On the main road about 1km (½ mile) west of the main site are the scant remains of the city's ancient **stadium** (stadio), where athletes performed on a U-shaped track before 6,000 spectators.

The **Sanctuary of Apollo Ylatis Hylates** (Ieron Apollonos Ylatou; daily, June–Aug 8am–7.30pm, Apr–May and Sept–Oct 8am–6pm, Nov–Mar 8am–5pm; charge) is to the west. Apollo was worshipped here as god of the woodlands as early as the 8th century BC, but most of the present structures were put up around AD100, and destroyed in the earthquake of 365.

From the guardian's lodge, take the path west to the pilgrims' entrance (through the stumpy remains of the Pafos Gate). The buildings here were probably hostels and storehouses for worshippers' votive offerings. The surplus was carefully placed in the *vothros* pit (at the centre of the site), which was full of terracotta figurines, mostly horse riders – still intact when uncovered by the archaeologists. Follow the path along the sanctuary's main street to the Temple of Apollo, which has been partially reconstructed to look as it did in AD100.

West to the Rock of Aphrodite

If the flat, hard-packed sands of Curium Beach don't appeal to you, try the coarse sand and shingle of Avdimou Beach, about 10km (6 miles) further west. But if you crave the creature comforts of a resort, then continue on to **Pissouri**. Note that the signs you see to both Avdimou and Pissouri are to the inland villages, not the beaches; follow instead the signs for Avdimou Beach or Pissouri Bay, which later changes to 'K. Pissouri' (short for Kato, or Lower Pissouri), then finally to 'Pissouri Jetty'. The latter is an attractive, sheltered place, with a coarse sand-and-shingle beach.

It is easy to be sceptical about a few rocks in the sea that are claimed to be the birthplace of a goddess, but this stretch of coast and the **Petra tou Romiou** rock formation, better known as the **Rock of Aphrodite**, is a beautiful natural feature. (The Greek name, 'Rock of Romios', has nothing to do with Aphrodite, but commemorates the Byzantine hero Romios.) He must also have been endowed with supernatural powers, as he is said to have used the huge rocks as missiles to ward off Arab raiders. The views east, away from the rocks to the dazzling white cliffs, are spectacular. Opposite the rocks, there is a parking and café. The water here is clear and inviting.

Petra tou Romiou, where Aphrodite first emerged from the sea

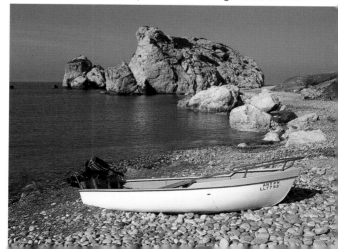

TROODOS MOUNTAINS

The **Troodos Mountains** (Vouna tou Troodou) in central Cyprus are the island's principal upland (note that it is pronounced more 'tro-dos', than 'true-doss'). They provide many things: a breath of fresh air for hot and flustered visitors and locals, a splendid collection of tiny Byzantine churches scattered around the hillsides, wonderful walking trails and, most importantly, much of the island's fresh water.

The roads climb through foothills with rushing streams and orchards, past villages perched on the slopes, surrounded at higher altitudes by pine forest. Monks and Greek-Cypriot EOKA fighters have also found refuge here, and the monasteries have been joined by resort hotels and spas, with even a little winter skiing near the resort of Troodos. On the southern slopes, above the 1,000m (3,300ft) line, are the vineyards and

Typical village in the Troodos Mountains

villages that produce Cyprus' highly regarded, sweet red dessert wine, Commandaria.

Platres to Troodos

Moufflon, or wild mountain sheep, thrive in the Troodos

At an altitude of 1,128m (3,700ft), **Pano Platres** is a good base for visiting the whole Troodos region. The little town occupies a charming and shady mountain site and features several hotels, restaurants and shops. The most popular pastime here is walking, and the Cyprus Tourism Organisation has marked several mountain trails, aimed at most ability levels. Stop at the Platres office for details. The most popular excursion is the 2km (1-mile) walk to the pretty **Kalidonia Falls**. The walk starts at the Psilo Dhendhro restaurant and trout farm just outside Platres (see pages 107–8), and is well marked.

Some 4km (2½ miles) from Platres is **Foini**, famous for its red-clay ceramics. You can see this craft being practised at home by a couple of local women who will be happy to let you watch them work. Foini also has a small folklore museum attached to a pottery workshop.

Omodos, renovated as a Troodos showpiece village, lies 6km (4 miles) south of Foini. It's an attractive place, but has become over-commercialised, and the tour buses diminish the atmosphere their occupants have come to savour. However, you can still find peace and quiet in the village's monastery of **Timios Stavros** (True Cross), which contains a memorial to EOKA.

It seems that all roads in the mountains lead to the eponymous resort of **Troodos**, which at 1,676m (5,500ft) is the

Old Kakopetria

island's highest. In the winter it has decent ski slopes, while in spring and autumn it's a good starting point for dedicated ramblers. Avoid midsummer when its main street turns into an overcrowded promenade of kitsch stalls and rumbling tour buses. A **visitor centre**, near the Dolphin restaurant, helps orientate visitors to the high mountains, and provides maps and information on the local wildlife and plants.

Rather than hiking, you may prefer to drive above the town to **Mt Olympos** (1,951m/6,401ft), Cyprus' tallest peak, also known locally as Khionistra (Snow-Tipped). For security reasons, you have to walk the last few hundred metres up to the giant British 'golf ball' radar installation on the summit; and the views are not that great. It's much better to gird your loins and tackle one of two nature trails – the Atalante or the Artemis – that circle the summit.

Kakopetria

In recent times, the Cyprus government has been investing in the reconstruction of traditional village houses as part of its plan to staunch the population flow from the hill villages to the coastal resorts and towns. And in few places is this effort more to be admired than in old **Kakopetria**. This historic part of town is more or less one long narrow street that runs parallel to the leafy river. The houses with balconies are being restored to bring out the subtle russet, amber and silver hues of the local stone and, with their log-cabin stores, have a real alpine feel. The town's tour de force is its beautifully restored **wooden mill**. The upper floor of the old flour mill is now home to The Mill restaurant *(see page 107)*, while the rest of the building has been turned into a hotel.

Just outside the village is one of the Troodos Mountains' famous frescoed churches *(see below)*, **Agios Nikolaos tis Stegis** (St Nicholas of the Roof; Tue–Sat 9am–4pm, Sun 11am– 4pm; free but donation appreciated). The name refers to the upper roof of shingles, which was built in the 13th century to shelter the older domed roof of tiles. Inside, the oldest frescoes date from the church's foundation in the 11th century.

Frescoed Churches

The Troodos Mountains' remarkable painted churches were built mostly between the 11th and the 16th centuries. For visitors, the astonishing degree of preservation and the striking beauty of the artwork makes for compulsive viewing. For scholars, the churches provide a fascinating lesson on the history of sacred art, a fact that has been officially recognised by Unesco (10 Troodos churches are on their World Cultural Heritage list). But it's also worth remembering that the primary function of the art was to act as a religious cartoon strip, teaching the simple, illiterate and often isolated parishioners the lessons of the Gospels.

The finest concentration of painted churches is in the northeastern part of the Troodos, where Panagia tis Asinou *(see page 42)*, Agios Nikolaos tis Stegis (in Kakopetria), Panagia tis Podythou (in Galata) and the outstanding Panagia tou Araka (in Lagoudera) are all within a short drive of each other. If a church is closed, you will have to trace the key-holder, usually the parish priest. Details are sometimes posted on the church door; otherwise ask at the nearest café for assistance.

Off the eastern edge of the Troodos, at Palaichori, you'll find the latest addition to the roster of Unesco mountain churches, **Metamorfosis tou Sotiros** (Transfiguration of the Saviour; no fixed times; free but donation appreciated), dating from the early 16th-century. Among its frescoes is a fine representation of the transfiguration of Jesus.

Galata

Just north of Kakopetria, **Galata** has a Unesco-listed 16th-century church. Heading north out of town, drive slowly and you will spot **Panagia tis Podythou** (daily 10am–1pm and 2–5pm; free but donation appreciated). It is not as well preserved, nor is the artwork as detailed as at some Troodos churches, but it still has some outstanding images. If it is closed the key-holder is usually somewhere between here and the smaller church of Archangelos, also known as **Panagia Theotokos** (Mary Mother of God), nearby. In Galata itself there is a small folk-art museum and a restored Ottoman *han* (inn).

Frescoed dome in the church at Lagoudera

If you've developed a taste for these mountain churches, continue east to **Lagoudera**, ◀ ㉑ where you will find **Panagia tou Araka** (Our Lady of the Wild Vetch), another fine example, with frescoes dating from 1192.

Heading in the opposite direction, the road west from Troodos winds through pine groves, vineyards and orchards of apples, pears, peaches, cherries, almonds and walnuts to **Prodromos**, 1,400m (4,600ft) above sea level. Its modest hotels and

Unesco's frescoes

Pedoulas has a Unesco-listed church, the 15th-century Archangelos Michail, which occupies an impressive site above the valley and features some remarkable frescoes.

restaurants are popular with hikers and jeep safaris. Further on is **Pedoulas**, famous for its cherries. In spring the locals flock here to see thousands of trees in blossom.

West to Kykkos

The monastery of **Panagia tou Kykkou** (Our Lady of Kykkos; monastery: daily dawn–dusk; free but donation appreciated; museum: daily, June–Oct 10am–6pm, Nov–May 10am–4pm; charge), 20km (12 miles) from Pedoulas, sits proudly remote from the world on a mountainside surrounded by pine forest. The drive offers marvellous views of the mountains at every twist and turn.

Kykkos is the richest and most important monastery on the island. Founded in 1094 by a hermit, it grew in prestige when Emperor Alexis Comnenos gave it a rich land grant and an icon of the Virgin Mary said to have been painted by St Luke. Having survived several fires, the icon is now covered in gilded silver. Its legendary rain-making powers still bring in farmers to pray in times of drought. Offerings left here range from jewellery to simple *ex votos* of beeswax.

If you come at a busy time, you may be dismayed to see a long queue of people waiting to enter the church. These will be Cypriots who wish to pass directly in front of the iconostasis, kissing the images to show their piety. Other visitors can enter the church via the rear door. The usual reaction to the

Kykkos Monastery

intense glitter and exuberant ornamentation of the church is one of astonishment. In fact, apart from the precious icon and a few other pieces, there is little of historical value here, since the monastery has been levelled by fire on four occasions – the first in 1365, the last in 1813 – and its buildings are no older than the early 19th century. Recently, they have been covered by scores of glittering new mosaics, though the real jewel in the crown is the museum. Here in cool and calm, you can learn about the history of the foundation and see some of its finest treasures.

Kykkos is also famous for having had Archbishop Makarios among its novices (he is buried on a hill above the monastery). In the 1950s, Kykkos was reputed to have served as a communications and supply base for the EOKA movement, and so became a symbol of the Cypriot nationalist struggle *(see page 23)*. On the road to the monastery, you will see brown-and-white tourist signs pointing to old EOKA hideouts.

West of Kykkos, rough mountain tracks and hard-surfaced roads lead downhill into the **Pafos Forest** (Dasos tis Pafou) and pass through **Cedar Valley** (Koilada tou Kedron), one of the highlights of the island's reforestation project. This steep-sided ravine hosts some 50,000 indigenous cedar trees *(Cedrus brevifolia)* and, in the surrounding forests of the rugged **Tripilos-Mavroi Gremmoi Nature Reserve** (Epifylaksi Fysis), the formerly endangered Cypriot wild mountain sheep, the moufflon, roam free.

PAFOS AND THE WEST

Once a sleepy fishing port, **Pafos** has been transformed into ◄ 23 a booming resort town. But visitors who want more than just sun and sand have plenty to occupy them. Pafos was the island's Roman-era capital and has a wealth of historic sites. It is also a good base for exploring nearby mountain villages and the nature trails of the Akamas Peninsula.

Legend attributes the founding of Palaia (Old) Pafos to the priest-king Cinyras, and the city-kingdom gained renown as the centre of Aphrodite's cult. The last king of Palaia Pafos, Nicocles, established the port of Nea (New) Pafos in the 4th century BC, though Palaia Pafos remained the centre of Aphrodite worship until the 4th century AD. Within 100 years of its founding, Nea Pafos surpassed Salamis as the chief city of Cyprus. However, earthquakes in 332 and 342 and Arab

Fishing boats in Pafos harbour

attacks in the 7th century forced most of the population inland to Ktima. For centuries, Pafos languished as a miserable, unsanitary seaport. However, the population gradually rose to over 2,000 by the late 19th century. It continued to grow and prosper, and despite some damage during the 1974 war, it bounced back– the boom after the opening of Pafos International Airport in 1985 attracting not only tourists but also new Cypriot settlers.

Kato Pafos

Kato (Lower) Pafos, along the seaside, is where most visitors stay, and is heavily developed. But the harbour still provides a picturesque haven for fishing and sailing boats as it curves around a jetty to the old **Pafos Fort** (Kastro tis Pafou; daily, Apr–May and Sept–Oct 8am–6pm, June–Aug 8am–7.30pm, Nov–Mar 8am–5pm; charge). Over the centuries, the fort has been a feudal castle, Turkish tower and British salt warehouse (scattered remains of an earlier Roman and Byzantine fort lie nearby). It's now an empty shell but worth the entrance fee for its rooftop views.

Just across the harbour car park are several of Pafos' ancient monuments, in an

Map labels

Cami Kehir (Great Mosque)

Covered Market

Hamam (Turkish Bath)

Pegeia

Polis

KTIMA

L.E. Palikaridi

Kinyra

Lemesos

L. Geo. Griva Digeni

Dimos (Town Hall)

Palati Episkopiko (Bishop's Palace)

Tachydromeio (Post Office)

Ethnografiko Mouseio (Ethnographical Museum)

Archaiologiki Mouseio Eparchias Pafou (Pafos District Archaeological Museum)

Talon ton Vasileon (Tombs of the Kings)

Leoforos Apostolou Pavlou

Agapinoros

Priamou

Talon ton Vasileon

Lysos Fabrica (Fabrica Hill)

Agios Agapitikos (St of Love)

Ikarou

Agia Solomoni

Boreiodytiki Pyli (Northwest Gate)

KATO PAFOS

Faros (Lighthouse)

Odeion (Odeon)

Frankish Baths

Agia Kyriaki (St Kyriaki)

Saranda Kolones

Psifidota tis Pafou (Pafos Mosaics)

Spiti tou Dionysou

Poseidonos

Geroskipou Beach

Spiti tou Aion

Spiti tou Thisea

Customs

Harbour

Spiti tou Orfea

Amfiteatro (Amphitheatre)

Kastro tis Pafou (Pafos Fort)

0   250 m
0   250 yds

Pafos

area that is now an archaeological park. The first, iden-
tified by its trademark arch,
is the ruin that's known as
Saranta Kolones (Forty
Columns), named after the
number of granite columns
found lying around here. Excavations have established its
identity as a French crusader
castle built at the end of the
12th century and destroyed
by an earthquake in 1222.

The ruins of Saranta Kolones

With the harbour on your left, walk towards the large, modern shed-like building in the distance. Sheltered beneath are
the famous **Pafos Mosaics** (Psifidota tis Pafou; daily, Apr–May
and Sept–Oct 8am–6pm, June–Aug 8am–7.30pm, Nov–Mar
8am–5pm; charge). These splendid decorative floors were
uncovered in the remains of luxurious Roman villas (3rd century AD) of Nea Pafos. The 'houses' are named after the
mosaics' most prominent motifs. The **House of Dionysos** displays the god of wine returning from India on a chariot drawn
by two panthers. This and other scenes, such as Dionysos
counselling moderation to the nymph Acme drinking wine
from a bowl, and Icarius of Athens getting shepherds drunk
with their first taste of wine, were customary decorations for
the dining room. The **House of Aion** has a spectacular five-
panelled mosaic. Its large central panel depicts Aion, god of
eternity, judging a beauty contest between a smug-looking
Queen Cassiopeia (the winner) and the unhappy, prettier
Nereides water nymphs. There are two more villas open to the
public, the **Villa of Theseus** and the **House of Orpheus**.

A short walk north leads to the restored **Odeon** (Odeion),
a small theatre dating from the 2nd century AD, built en-

Pafos is famed for its Roman mosaics

tirely of hewn limestone blocks. In a picturesque hillside setting, it seats 1,250 spectators for musical and theatrical performances held regularly in the summer.

Kato Pafos to Ktima

From the road entrance to the harbour, Leoforos Apostolou Pavlou climbs towards the excavated site of a 4th-century AD Christian basilica known as **Agia Kyriaki** (Saint Kyriaki). Amid the ruins of the seven-aisled church, you can make out mosaic pavements with floral and geometric patterns, Corinthian capitals and columns of green-and-white marble imported from Greece. Arabic graffiti on the columns dates from the invasion that destroyed the basilica in 653. One of the columns is called **St Paul's Pillar**, to which the apostle was (apocryphally) tied and lashed 39 times for preaching the Gospel. Amid the ruins is the handsome post-Byzantine **Panagia Chrysopolitissa** (Our Lady of the Golden City) church (sometimes also referred to as Agia Kyriaki). Just north of the site are the tiny, ruined, twin-domed Frankish Baths (Loutra ton Fragkon), with an ancient gnarled tree pushing up through the masonry.

A little further up the hill is the intriguing sight of a tree festooned with hundreds of handkerchiefs and rags. It marks the **Catacomb of Agia Solomoni** (Katakombi tou Agiou Solomoni), once regarded as a spot where disease could be cured by miracles, and still doing a good trade with believers today. The tradition of tying a handkerchief to a tree at a sacred site is common in the Near and Middle East. The handkerchief is given as a votive offering (akin to lighting a candle in a church in the West to accompany a prayer of thanks or devotion), and goes back to the days when handkerchiefs were valuable items.

Northwest of what was Nea Pafos is the ancient community's necropolis, known as the **Tombs of the Kings** (Tafon ton Vasileon; daily, June–Aug 8am–7.30pm, Apr–May and Sept–Oct 8am–6pm, Nov–Mar 8am–5pm; charge). The title is a misnomer, as the subterranean burial chambers were built from the 3rd century BC to the 3rd century AD, when Pafos had no kings. But many of the tombs are imposing enough to suggest they were at least the resting places of important officials. This 'city of the dead' is an imitation of the city of the living, thus giving an insight into the architecture of Nea Pafos: spacious courtyards with Doric columns and decorative entablatures. It is fun to explore (tombs 3, 4 and 8 are the best), but do be careful as there are unprotected drops.

Within the Tombs of the Kings

Ktima

Set on a hilltop above the resort, the upper part of Pafos known as **Ktima** is a breath of fresh air and everyday reality. There is a colourful daily produce market and a variety of souvenir stalls. After shopping, you can sit down for a drink or a meal and enjoy the excellent views of the coast.

There are two small museums in the centre of Ktima. The **Ethnographic Museum** (Ethnografiko Mouseio), also known as the Eliades Collection, on Odos Exo Vrisis (Mon–Sat 9.30am–5pm, Sun 10am–2pm; charge), is set in a charming 19th-century house. It combines prehistoric fossils, classical antiquities and Cypriot folklore of the 18th and 19th centuries. In the garden, burial chambers from the 3rd century BC have been uncovered. Across the road, in a wing of the **Bishop's Palace**, is the **Byzantine Museum** (Byzantino Mouseio; Mon–Fri 9am–4pm, until 3pm in winter, Sat 9am–1pm; charge), a gallery of icons salvaged from local chapels.

You'll need transport to reach the **Pafos District Archaeological Museum** (Archaiologiko Mouseio Eparchias Pafou; Tue–Fri 8am–3pm, Thur until 5pm, Sat 9am–3pm; charge), which is on the road to Limassol. It houses some remarkable sculptures found in the Villa of Theseus *(see page 71)*, including a statue of Asclepios (the Greek master of medicine) feeding an egg to the snake coiled around his staff. Also, look out for the pottery hot-water bottles from the 1st century AD, specially moulded to fit all parts of the body.

South of Pafos

Just southeast of Pafos is the village of **Geroskipou**, which comes from *Hieros Kipos*, meaning 'Sacred Garden' of Aphrodite. Pilgrims would stop here on their way to the goddess's temple at Palaia Pafos. The 11th-century church of **Agia Paraskevi** (Saint Paraskevi) in Geroskipou is a rare island example of a five-domed basilica. Inside are some 15th-century

murals and a much-revered icon from the same period, with a
Virgin and Child on one side and a *Crucifixion* on the reverse.

In a restored house nearby is the informative **Folk Art
Museum** (Mouseio Laikis Technis Geroskipou; daily, Apr–
Oct 9am–5pm, Nov–Mar 8am–4pm; charge). Typical of a rich
Cypriot's villa in the 18th century, the upper storey is ringed
with handsome wooden balconies. Displays include gourds
made into unlikely items (such as swimming aids for children), domestic and farming implements, and rural costumes.

From here, continue southeast for about 12km (8 miles) and
turn off at **Kouklia**, once Palaia (Old) Pafos, where the cult
of Aphrodite was celebrated.
The rites of the love goddess
flourished at the **Sanctuary
of Aphrodite** (Iero tis Afroditis; Fri–Wed 9am–4pm, Thur
8am–5pm; charge). Alas, little romance can be found in
the ruins. Most of the valuable finds have been taken to
Nicosia, though a copy of the
famous mosaic of *Leda and
the Swan* remains in situ. The
sturdy Château de Covocle
(originally a Lusignan manor-
farm) is now home to the
Palaia Pafos Museum (same
hours as the Sanctuary; free).
Its prize exhibit is a large con-
ical stone that symbolised the
goddess (her beauty was too
great to represent literally)
and was the epicentre of
Aphrodite worship.

Remains of fluted columns at
the Sanctuary of Aphrodite

The monastery of Agios
Neofytos

North of Pafos

The beaches in Pafos are unremarkable, so many visitors travel 10km (6 miles) north to the better sands, plentiful watersports, and beachside dining at **Coral Bay** (Kolpos Korallion). A wave of development has replaced olive groves, orchards and banana plantations between here and the hilltop village of **Pegeia**. Further up the coast, the handsome little **Agios Georgios**, crowned by a clifftop church and an archaeological zone, is going the same way.

To the northeast, 10km (6 miles) from Pafos, the monastery of **Agios Neofytos** (St Neofytos; daily, Apr–Oct 9am–1pm and 2–6pm, Nov–Mar 9am–1pm and 2–4pm; monastery free, charge for museum and Hermitage) dominates a wooded slope. Its church has fine frescoes and icons, but the main focus is the 12th-century **Enkleistra** (Hermitage), around which the monastery grew. The saintly historian and theologian Neofytos (1134–1214) supposedly hacked this cave-dwelling out of the rock with his own hands and then supervised the creation of the frescoes that decorate the chapel and cell. One shows Neofytos himself, flanked by archangels Michael and Gabriel.

On the north coast, the small town of **Polis** stands where the ancient city-kingdom of Marion once boasted rich gold and copper mines. Archaeological finds from the site are on display at the **Marion-Arsinoe Archaeological Museum** (Archaiologiko Mouseio Marion-Arsinoi; Tue–Fri 8am–3pm, Thur until 5pm, Sat 9am–3pm; charge). The town centre has been restored and has a pleasant if touristy enclave of cafés and restaurants. Polis is a prelude to the fishing port and beach resort of **Lakki**. Restaurants, cafés and bars cluster around the picturesque harbour, flanked by sand and pebble beaches.

Romantics should head west to the end of the road. From here it's an easy five-minute walk to the **Baths of Aphrodite** (Loutra tis Afroditis), a small, shaded natural pool and springs set in a cool green glade, where the goddess was wont to bathe. Mere mortals are not allowed to cool off here, but nearby paths lead down to narrow pebble beaches with crystal-clear water.

Alternatively, if you want to go hiking, marked paths lead off into the **Akamas Peninsula** (Chersoniso tou Akama), one

A Wilderness Under Threat

Untamed and scenic, the Akamas Peninsula arouses strong passions, both among those who admire its beauty and wildlife, and among developers who see it as a potential paradise for upmarket tourists. Hikers, bird-watchers and nature-lovers relish the Akamas' rugged terrain. It is the last major piece of unspoilt coastline in South Cyprus. But commercial interests are encroaching, and there are proposals for luxury developments.

Organisations as disparate as the World Bank, the European Union, Friends of the Earth and Greenpeace have, for more than 20 years, called for the creation of a national park. The island's powerful developer lobby and many local residents oppose this, or at any rate prefer to have only limited protection for the area. In 2000, a government committee recommended 'mild and controlled' development in the Akamas and to reduce the area of the proposed national park by more than two-thirds.

The debate continues. Successive Cypriot governments have been reluctant to grasp what will surely turn out to be a hot potato, no matter which way they decide. Proposals put forward in 2005 seem to confirm the glacial drift towards 'controlled', 'mild' and 'legal' development around a reduced protected area, but no decision has been made.

The rugged landscape of the Akamas Peninsula

of the few unspoilt wildernesses left on the island and currently a battleground between environmentalists and developers *(see box, page 77)*. In a marine reserve at **Lara Bay** (Kolpos Laras), on the peninsula's west coast, endangered green and logger-head turtles come ashore to bury their eggs. Despite the threat of development elsewhere on the peninsula, the government has so far decided that this beach will remain untouched.

In the other direction from Polis, east along the coast, a scenic route leads through seafront villages that have, so far, been scarcely developed. The rugged promontory at **Pomos** is worth a stop, as are the beaches of nearby **Pachyammos**, in which village the large modern church of **Agios Rafail** (St Rafael) contains a suite of colourful murals. From here the road, climbing into the steep Tilliria hills, curves around the Turk-ish military enclave at Kokkina (Erenköy), before finishing at the bustling resort of **Kato Pyrgos**, right up against the Green Line (a crossing-point is due to open here at the end of 2009).

NORTHERN CYPRUS

The Turkish-occupied north, which comprises around 37 percent of the island, contains some of Cyprus' most beautiful landscapes, best beaches, most dramatic historical sites and two of its finest towns. Partition and the subsequent political isolation has helped preserve the countryside from the ravages of mass tourism.

It is possible to whizz around Northern Cyprus in a day and cover – or at least glimpse – all the main sights, although unless you are short on time, this is not recommended. In three days you can see the sights, including northern Nicosia (see pages 37–9), at a more leisurely pace.

Visiting the North

There are currently six crossing-points along the buffer zone that separates North and South. There are two crossings for pedestrians in central Nicosia: on Odos Lidras in the Old City (see page 37) and at the old Ledra Palace Hotel close to the Pafos Gate (see page 32). Border crossings for vehicles are at Agios Dometios (Metehan) in the western suburbs of Nicosia; at Pergamos (Beyarmudu) and Agios Nikolaos (Akyar) within the Dhekelia British Sovereign Base Area, close to Famagusta (Gazimağusa); and at Astromeritis-Kato Zodeia (Boştancı), close to Morfou (Güzelyurt). Further crossing-points are being negotiated, with one at Kato Pyrgos (Günebakan) on the north coast due to open by the end of 2009.

The procedure for crossing is straightforward, though since the border's opening in 2003 there have been crowds of visitors, and frequent queues. Officially the border opens at 8am and closes for returning visitors at midnight. The police may ask to see your passport. There is currently no limit on the number of times you may cross. EU citizens have the right of unrestricted movement throughout Cyprus; there may be restrictions for non-EU citizens, though these may not be enforced.

Pentadaktylos (Five Finger) Mountain

The Mountain Castles

North of Nicosia the terrain rises to the **Pentadaktylos** (Beş-parmak) **Mountains**, which Lawrence Durrell, who lived here from 1953 to 1956, described as 'the *par excellence* Gothic range for it is studded with crusader castles pitched on the dizzy spines of the mountains, commanding the roads which run over the saddles between'. The range's most striking peak is Pentadaktylos (Five Fingers).

The castles now lie in noble ruin, victims not of enemy bombardment but of demolition by the Venetians. Most spectacular is **Agios Ilarion** (St Hilarion; daily, summer 9am–5pm, winter 9am–1pm and 2–4.45pm; charge), which climbs along knife-edge ridges in three tiers of battlements and towers, reaching an altitude of 670m (2,200ft) under twin peaks, with steps leading up and down in all directions.

The castle was built in the 10th century around an earlier church and monastery honouring the hermit Hilarion, who fled here when the Arabs advanced on Syria. The original Byzantine structure was fortified and extended by the Lusignans as a summer residence. The views down to Keryneia harbour are superb and, on a clear day, you can see the mountains of southern Turkey some 100km (60 miles) away.

Another dramatic castle worth seeing is **Voufaventon** ('Buffeted by the Winds'), to the east. This is the island's highest fortress, at 954m (3,130ft), and is often shrouded in mist.

Keryneia (Girne)

Offering the most beautiful sheltered harbour in Cyprus and a grand old castle, the charming town of **Keryneia** – Girne in Turkish – is the most strikingly situated on the island. The venerable buildings that line the harbour have almost all been converted into bars or restaurants, but compared with the resorts on the south coast, Keryneia is still relaxed and understated.

29

Overlooking the harbour is the massive bulk of **Keryneia Castle** (daily, summer 9am–7pm, winter 9am–1pm and 2–4.45pm; charge), which dates mostly from the 15th century. Today, its walls enclose a Byzantine chapel, royal apartments and various historical displays, including the **Kyrenia ship**, one of the oldest vessels ever recovered from the sea (and featured on three of the Cypriot euro coins). This Greek trading ship sank near Cyprus around 300BC and was discovered in 1965 by a sponge diver. The surviving hull has been painstakingly preserved and is shown with part of its cargo.

Fisherman at Keryneia

In the foothills behind Keryneia are the ruins of the

Belapais Abbey

superbly sited Gothic abbey of **Belapais** (Beylerbeyi; daily summer 9am–7pm, winter 9am–1pm and 2–4.45pm; charge). Facing the sea, the 'Abbey of Peace' stands on a 30m (100ft) escarpment, its buildings enclosing cypresses, palms and orange trees. The abbey was built by the Lusignans and took on its present form in the 13th century. The elegant cloister is adorned with finely carved figures, while the splendid vaulted refectory has six bays and a fine rose window.

30

West of Keryneia

You can follow the line of the Pentadaktylos range west to their end, and continue on through the Lebanese Maronite village of **Kormakitis** (Koruçam) to the scenic tip of **Cape Kormakitis** (Akrotirio Kormakitis/Koruçam Burnu). Southward around the curve of Morfou Bay is the old bishop's seat of **Morfou** (Güzelyurt) and its venerable monastery of **Agios Mamas** (St Mamas; daily, summer 9am–7pm, winter 9am–1pm and 2–4.45pm; charge).

On the narrow strip of Northern Cyprus squeezed between the buffer zone and the sea lie the remains of the ancient (6th-century BC) Graeco-Roman town of **Soloi** (Soli; daily, summer 9am–7pm, winter 9am–1pm and 2–4.45pm; charge) and those of the Persian-era (5th-century BC) palace at **Vouni** (Vuni; daily, summer 10am–5pm, winter 9am–1pm and 2–4.45pm; charge).

The Karpasia Peninsula

If you have time (it's best not to try this on a day trip from the South) you can take a long, exhilarating drive east of Keryneia, all the way into the long 'panhandle' of the Karpasia (Karpaz) Peninsula. Along the way, a tree-shaded hiking trail leads from **Kalograia** (Esentepe) to the isolated (and no longer in use) 13th-century monastery and church of **Antifonitis** (the Proclaimer; daily, summer 9am–2pm, winter 9am–1pm and 2–4.45pm; charge), dedicated to the Archangel Michael. Though partially ruined and vandalized, both its situation and exceptional surviving frescoes make it a worthwhile stop.

Close to the peninsula's spray-tossed tip are the white-washed walls of the historic monastery of **Apostolos** **Andreas** (Apostle Andrew; daily summer 9am–7pm, winter 9am–1pm and 2–4.45pm; charge). Since 2003, pilgrims have been able to freely visit and pray for miracles at the icon of St Andrew in the monastery's 18th-century church.

Famagusta (Gazimağusa)

The east coast port of **Famagusta** (Ammochostos/Gazimağusa) was a mere village when Christian refugees arrived from Palestine in 1291. Soon it developed into a boom town of extravagant merchants and notorious courtesans, becoming one of the wealthiest cities in the world. It all ended in 1374 when the Genoese took the port amid much bloodshed. Worse was to come in 1571, with the Turkish invasion and the most famous siege in the island's history *(see page 19)*.

Othello's Tower, Famagusta

Famagusta rose again in the 20th century to become the most important port in Cyprus and a major tourist centre. But once again, in 1974, a Turkish invasion was to leave the city a mere shadow of its former self. Since the departure of the Greek Cypriots, **Varosha** (Varosia/Maraş), the pre-1974 beach resort area, is eerily deserted and decrepit. Yet the Venetian fortifications and old town are still of great interest.

Beside the harbour stands **Othello's Tower** (daily, summer 10am–7pm, winter 9am–1pm and 2–4.45pm; charge), named after a 16th-century governor of Cyprus, Christoforo Moro, sometimes cited as the model for Shakespeare's tormented Moor. Most formidable of the fortifications is the **Martinengo Bastion** in the northwest corner of the old town. Its walls, 4–6m (13–19ft) thick, provided stubborn resistance to the Turks during the siege of 1570–1.

Converted from a cathedral, Lala Mustafa Paşa Mosque

The town's many churches were founded by the Lusignans. The finest was St Nicholas' Cathedral, where the Lusignan kings were crowned as 'kings' of Jerusalem. It was converted into a mosque, the **Lala Mustafa Paşa Camii** (daily dawn–dusk), named after the commander of the Turkish invasion. The handsome structure was completed in 1326 with a majestic western façade worthy of any great European cathedral. Although the Turks stripped the interior of images of the human form, and there was damage from an earthquake in 1735, it can still be admired for its fine Gothic features.

Salamis

Overlooking the sea just 8km (5 miles) north of Famagusta, the ancient city of **Salamis** (daily, summer 9am–7pm, winter 9am–1pm and 2–4.45pm; charge) rivals Kourion *(see page 57)* as the island's finest archaeological site. For 2,000 years, Salamis competed with Pafos as the leading city in Cyprus and was a haven for Greek artists and intellectuals exiled from Athens. As Constantia, it became the capital of early-Christian Cyprus in AD350, subsequently suffering an earthquake and disappearing completely after the Arab invasion of 647.

The **Roman theatre** (theatrum) probably succeeded an earlier Greek structure and its 50-row auditorium – which is the largest in Cyprus – seated 15,000. Also impressive is the spacious **gymnasium**. The graceful Corinthian columns were brought here from the theatre and re-erected by the Byzantines. In the adjoining **public baths** (thermae), you can distinguish the *frigidarium, tepidarium* and *caldarium*. The water was channelled from Kythrea, 40km (25 miles) away, via a Roman aqueduct, parts of which are still standing.

Just west of Salamis is the monastery of **Apostolos Varna-vas** (Apostle Barnabas; daily, summer 9am–7pm, winter 9am–1pm and 2–4.45pm; charge). He accompanied Paul on his mission to Cyprus in AD45and was martyred in Salamis at the hands of Jews he was trying to convert. The saint's rock-cut burial chamber is now empty, but its discovery in AD478 helped the Church of Cyprus achieve autonomy within the Orthodox faith, and led to the building of the monastery nearby. The present drum-domed church was built in 1756 with elements from an earlier 15th-century church and columns and capitals from Salamis. It is now a museum of Byzantine icons.

WHAT TO DO

Cyprus offers plenty to do beyond sightseeing. Sporting activities benefit from a great climate and clear coastal waters, while entertainment ranges from some of the Mediterranean's hottest nightclubs in Agia Napa to more sedate folklore shows at local festivals, and even a play or concert in the grand setting of an ancient open-air amphitheatre.

SPORTS

The beaches may not all have the best sands, but they do have crystal-clear, unpolluted seas. Hikers can find solitude and marvellous scenery in the unspoilt Troodos and Pentadaktylos mountains, and on the rugged Akamas Peninsula and the gentler Karpasia Peninsula.

Watersports

Scuba divers and **snorkellers** are major beneficiaries of Cyprus' limpid seas. In water temperatures ranging from 16°C (60°F) to 27°C (80°F), you can explore submerged cliffs, valleys and caves, and get close-up views of sea anemones and sponges, exotic coloured fish and crustaceans (although marine life is not abundant in the nutrient-poor eastern Mediterranean). You can also dive on several wrecks, including the ferry *Zenobia*, which sank off Larnaka in 1980. You will find diving centres with equipment for hire and instruction at Pafos, Coral Bay, Lakki, Larnaka, Limassol, Agia Napa and Protaras in the South, and at Keryneia (Girne) in the North.

Windsurfing and **water-skiing** are widely available, with equipment for hire at public and hotel beaches. Other

Parasailing off the beach at Agia Napa

Clear water allows for great snorkelling

activities such as **jet-skiing** and **parasailing** are available at the main resorts. Those serious about **sailing** can hire craft from the harbours at Agia Napa, Pafos, Lakki, Larnaka, Limassol and Keryneia.

Golf
Golf is not a game much associated with Cyprus, but four excellent courses are well worth seeking out: **Secret Valley**, tucked away in a lovely hidden location not far from Aphrodite's Birthplace; **Aphrodite Hills** close by; **Tsada**, northeast of Pafos; and **Vikla**, near Limassol. The North has courses at Pentageia (Yeşilyurt) and Agios Amvrosios (Esentepe).

Walking and Hiking
The Troodos Mountains, Pentadaktylos Mountains and Akamas Peninsula are ideal for hiking, though for many people it will be too strenuous, or just plain uncomfortable, in sum-

mer. If you want to go it alone, the Cyprus Tourism Organisation has maps and information on local itineraries *(see pages 131–2)*. Visit the Pafos or Polis offices for the Akamas Peninsula, the Pano Platres office for the Troodos Mountains and the Keryneia (Girne) tourist office for the Pentadaktylos, or ask at any CTO office for the excellent *Nature Trails* brochure, which maps out walks all over the south of the island. Adjacent to the Baths of Aphrodite car park, there's a CTO tourist pavilion that has details of walking trails; it is from here that paths lead off into the Akamas.

For organised trekking tours of the Akamas, try the well-respected Exalt Travel (tel: 2531 5154). Their adventurous programme takes in dry river beds, lunar landscapes of chalk plateau, refreshing waterfalls and the spectacular Avakas Gorge. You don't need to be experienced, as long as you are reasonably healthy and have a decent pair of walking shoes.

Experienced hikers in search of adventure in the Troodos may enjoy the nature trails that go from the forestry station of **Stavros tis Psokas**, northwest of Kykkos. There

On Two Wheels

Fancy a spot of mountain-biking? Cyprus has the mountains, and you can hire bikes in all the main resorts. There's little to stop you – except the fact that the mountains are dauntingly high and steep, it's going to be hot up there and the steed you're riding will probably look as if it went through Cyprus with Richard the Lionheart.

If you're sure you can hack it, there's plenty of testing terrain in the Troodos and Pentadaktylos Mountains, on the Akamas Peninsula, around Cape Gkreko and in the wilds of Tilliria, Pitsilia and Karpasia. Take plenty of water and don't overdo it in summer. Anyone of a less rugged disposition can content themselves with a relaxing cycle along the many quiet, smooth and mostly flat farm roads close to the sea.

Winter sports

Sporting activities are not limited to the summer on the island. In winter, lifts provide access to four ski runs on Mt Olympos, and cross-country skiing is possible. Depending on snow conditions (which are usually poor), the ski season runs from January to late March.

is a hostel here that you need to reserve in advance (tel: 2699 9144). Less intimidating are the Atalante and Artemis trails (12km/8 miles and 7km/4 miles respectively) around Mt Olympos *(see page 64)* just below the summit. An easy but rewarding trek will lead you to the Kalidonia Falls *(see page 63)*.

Extreme Sports

You can augment the hazards of partying in Agia Napa with **bungee-jumping** at nearby Nissi Beach: the drop is 60m (200ft). Then there is the **Slingshot**, also in Agia Napa, claimed to be the highest and fastest ride in the world. Riders are propelled to a height of 100m (300ft) in a breathtaking 1.3 seconds.

SHOPPING

The quality of many tourist shops in Cyprus is low, tending towards cheap, imported tat. Instead you should head for the nearest **Cyprus Handicraft Service** (CHS) shop, showcasing the best of the island's artisans. Compared with elsewhere, goods here are expensive, but they are handmade and have the CHS label to guarantee it. You will find CHS shops at – **Pafos**: 64 Leoforos Apostolou Pavlou; **Limassol**: 25 Odos Themidou; **South Nicosia**: CHS workshop, 186 Leoforos Athalassis; **Larnaka**: 6 Odos Kosma Lysioti. You can also find the works of talented craftspeople in various fields in their own shops and in outlets that stock quality products.

Best Buys

Basketry. The choice ranges from small baskets in decorative shapes and colours to large articles in rush or cane.

Brass. Look for candlesticks, ashtrays, small boxes, religious ornaments and trays.

Ceramics. Most ceramics are crude and garish. Seek out artisans who look back to antiquity for inspiration, creating charming animal figurines, little vessels and terracotta statuettes. The functional wares from Kornos and Foini include attractive hand-made wine and oil jars (most of them too large to carry).

Copperware. After 3,000 years, the copper industry remains a source of Cypriot pride. There are all manner of hand-crafted wares, including pots, saucepans and bowls.

Colourful ceramic souvenirs

Embroidery. The island's most important cottage industry items are fine linen tablecloths, doilies, runners and handkerchiefs, stitched with the intricate geometric patterns of *lefkaritika* from Lefkara, and the more colourful *pafitika* from Pafos.

Food and wine. A sweet, jelly-like confection, *loukoúmi*, or 'Cyprus Delight', is a speciality of Geroskipou, near Pafos. The Turkish version, *lokum*, or 'Turkish Delight', is sold in the North. You may also want to take home olives or sealed packets of *halloúmi* cheese. Of the many wines and liqueurs pro-

Terracotta urns for sale

duced in Cyprus, the most popular gift is the sweet red dessert wine Commandaria.

Icons. Pieces available range from exquisite works produced by highly skilled nuns and monks, such as Brother Kallinikos *(see page 48)*, to the cheaper items on sale in most gift shops.

Jewellery. You can find good quality silver and gold, the latter is almost always 18-carat, but in the resorts the quality can be poor. Good jewellers will provide a certificate of authenticity.

Leather goods. Manufactured locally, shoes and sandals are reasonably priced in Cyprus.

ENTERTAINMENT

Most resorts have a tourist-office brochure or a privately produced publication listing what's on. Another good resource is the What's On sections of the *Cyprus Mail* and *Cyprus Weekly* in the South, and of *Cyprus Today* in the North.

Folklore Shows

Many hotels offer weekly folklore shows with costumed performers singing and dancing to traditional Greek tunes. Visitors are encouraged to get up and dance along. Many tavernas also have Greek Cypriot and Greek dancing on a regular basis.

One local speciality is the glass-balancing routine. A dancer will have an empty glass placed upside down on his head and will dance a few steps to show his balancing agility. It may not be terribly impressive with just one glass, but by the time his colleagues have balanced a 30-glass tower, the crowd is open-mouthed. Another routine involves placing a glass half-full of water into an old-fashioned wooden sieve. The sieve is at first gently swung from side to side, then furiously rotated while the dancer spins like a whirling dervish. The glass and liquid remain in place, and the audience stays dry.

In Northern Cyprus, you may find (and be invited to engage in) belly dancing, and can enjoy Turkish music from enthusiastic if not always terribly talented local combos.

Historic Venues

The most memorable and distinctive evening's entertainment on offer is a night at the ancient theatre. The **Pafos Odeon** stages plays (in English), and the magnificently situated theatre at **Kourion** is a wonderful place to catch a Shakespeare play or classical drama, or to hear some jazz. If you are staying in Limassol, or even Pafos, it's well worth the effort to get there. Hire a cushion, or take along something soft to sit

Nightlife and Agia Napa

Agia Napa (see page 50) is one of the Mediterranean's major party destinations for young holidaymakers. It has a number of clubbing options, from '80s-revival nights to the latest in hardcore sounds. In July and August the crowd is very much 18–30 and can get a bit rowdy at times. However, the authorities operate a zero tolerance policy towards drugs and raucous behaviour, which, for some, has spelled the end of the party. Outside the high season, you will find older, more discerning tastes being catered for.

The popular clubs change from season to season, so ask around, but places like The Castle Club, Starskys, Abyss, and Black and White seem able to keep up. And don't go out too early – the real action doesn't start until around 1am. Although not so well known as Agia Napa's, both Pafos and Limassol have their own club and nightlife scenes.

Rockpooling on Nissa Beach

on. Out of high season, you might need a sweater, too. Another pleasant historic outdoor venue is the castle at **Larnaka**, with performances of dance and theatre during the Larnaka Festival in July.

CHILDREN'S CYPRUS

With clean beaches and endless sunshine, Cyprus is great for children (but be sure to protect them from the fierce Mediterranean sun). Cypriots, like most southern Europeans, love children and there are few, if any, restrictions on where they can go.

If the kids are bored with the beach, but not with the water, there are four water parks to experience. **WaterWorld**, just outside Agia Napa at Agia Thekla, claims to be the biggest water theme park in Europe. It has over 20 rides, ranging from high-speed thrill chutes to the Lazy River. Greek columns, statues and fountains provide the theme. There are three other water parks: **Wet 'n' Wild**, just east of Limassol, is larger and wilder than **Watermania** on the western side of Limassol at Fassouri. The **Paphos Aphrodite Waterpark** between Pafos and Geroskipou also has its superlatives, including a long rafting ride and a plunging descent called the Kamikazi.

The biggest and best amusement park is **La Luna Fun Fair** in Agia Napa. Kids will also enjoy a chance to view the underwater world from a **glass-bottomed boat**, such as the 30-seat **Yellow Submarine** which operates from Agia Napa. **Go-karts** and **horse-riding** are also available at the main resorts.

Festivals and Holy Days

January *Fota*. On Epiphany Day (6 January), bishops bless the waters in all the seaside towns, throwing Limassol's Holy Crosses into the sea. Youngsters dive for them.

February/March *Carnival*. Limassol's 10-day long celebration features fancy-dress balls and a spate of parades. It's not Rio, but it's fun.

March/April *Good Friday*. Solemn Orthodox Masses take place all over Cyprus, with a procession of the Holy Sepulchre along main thoroughfares. *Easter*. A midnight service takes place on the Saturday before Easter, when people light their candles from the priest's, moving around the church and chanting the litany. Once the service is over, spectacular firework displays begin. On Easter Sunday, high Masses celebrate the resurrection of Christ.

May/June *Kataklysmos*. The Festival of the Flood coincides with Pentecost, and this two-day holiday harks back to ancient times, when Cypriots convened at temples to worship and sacrifice to Adonis and Aphrodite. Today, there are excursions to the beach, parties, games, colourful parades and competitions – especially in Pafos.

Nicosia International Arts Festival. This two-week event in June features everything from art exhibits and folk dancing to avant-garde ballet and rock concerts.

Ancient Greek Drama Festival. This festival of classical Greek theatre takes place between June and August. Plays are performed on warm summer evenings against the spectacular backdrops of the island's ancient open-air amphitheatres, such as the ones at Pafos and Kourion.

July *Larnaka Festival*. During this historically oriented festival, dance and theatre performances are staged at the castle in Larnaka.

August *Assumption of the Virgin*. On 15 August, the faithful gather at the leading monasteries and churches. This is the most important day in the Greek religious festival calendar. Beware – the crowds are massive.

September *Limassol* Wine Festival. A fortnight of wine-tastings, dancing and folklore shows. (Note that this event may begin in late August.)

Agia Napa Festival. This well-established festival of folklore, music, dance and theatre attracts large crowds.

EATING OUT

The food of Cyprus will be familiar to anyone who has visited Greece (or, in the case of Northern Cyprus, Turkey). Basically, it comprises grilled meats and fish, salads and a small selection of speciality casseroles. Strangely, fresh vegetables, though grown in abundance on the island, don't always find their way on to restaurant tables.

At its best, Cypriot cooking is simple, hearty and healthy. Unfortunately, with mass tourism has come that bland hybrid called 'international cuisine', and worse still, mass catering has impacted badly on the local food. Bright-pink factory-produced *taramasalata* and imitation crab sticks are now passed off in some places as part of a traditional fish *meze* (see page 99).

Where to Eat

Many tourist-orientated restaurants now cook to a price, and if you are at all serious about your food, you should choose very carefully where you eat. During the summer season, restaurants that are open all day generally operate from 9.30am–11pm. Those that only serve lunch and dinner are usually open noon–3pm and 6.30–11.30pm. If you are planning a special journey to a restaurant in low season, it's advisable to call ahead to confirm opening hours, as some places close early or open late out of season.

Some traditional tavernas have no menu, just a set meal, and you pay a fixed price for whatever is being

New creations

For the latest thing, look for sophisticated restaurants serving 'New Cypriot Cuisine', reinterpreting the old standards in new and intriguing ways, and adding touches of international fusion.

A classic Greek salad

served that night. Trust them and enjoy your meal. Cypriots are known for their generosity, and restaurateurs are no exception. In a good local restaurant, fresh fruit, Greek coffee, perhaps even the local wine, may well be on the house. You should return the gesture with a generous tip.

Note that the terms *taverna* and restaurant are often used loosely in Cyprus, though the former implies an informal, even rustic traditional eating and drinking establishment.

Fast Food and Starters

Cypriot fast food generally means a *pita* bread stuffed with *sheftalia* (a kind of sausage) or *souvláki*, a kebab of grilled cubes of fresh lamb or goat, plus salad, and a yogurt dressing. The ingredients will be fresh and the *sheftalia* home-made, with local herbs. You'll get these snacks at small takeaways or cafés. They are the cheapest and arguably one of the healthiest ways of filling up.

Dining in Nicosia old town

Common to nearly all restaurants serving Cypriot-style food are four dips: *taramasalata*, a pink fish-roe paste made with olive oil and lemon juice, and thickened with mashed potato or softened bread; *talatoura*, a Cypriot variant of the Greek *tzatziki* (yoghurt with cucumber, crushed garlic and fresh mint); *tahini*, a sesame-seed paste with garlic; and *hummus*, puréed chick-peas, olive oil and spices. To accompany these dips, you will be served either fresh Cypriot sesame-seed bread *(koulouri)* or *pita* bread.

Koupépia, is another well-known starter, also known as *dolmádes* or *dolmadaki* – vine leaves stuffed with rice and lamb, flavoured with mint. Another Greek staple, stuffed vegetables, is not particularly common in Cyprus. Two more permanent items on the starter section of a menu are *loúnza*, a thinly sliced fillet of smoked pork, and *halloúmi*, a Cypriot ewe's-milk cheese. Both of these may be served hot (chargrilled or fried) or cold, and are often offered as a combination. Much less commonly found on restaurant menus is *loukanika*, a Cypriot smoked sausage.

Local soups are not common on menus (apart from the ubiquitous vegetable soup, which is usually made from leftovers). But if you do get the chance, try *avgolemono*, a lemon-flavoured chicken broth thickened with egg and served with rice. Another rarity to look out for is *kypriakes ravioles*, Cypriot ravioli stuffed with *halloúmi*, eggs and mint.

Meat Dishes and Vegetables

Almost without exception, every restaurant that serves Greek-Cypriot food in the tourist resorts has a section on its menu entitled Cypriot Specialities. Invariably, it includes the following dishes: *moussaka*, a layered dish of minced meat, aubergine and potatoes, with a bechamel sauce and spices; *afelia*, a tender pork stew made with red wine, cumin and coriander seeds; *kléftiko*, oven-roasted lamb with mint, the traditional Sunday lunch for the locals; *stifádo*, a catch-all term for a stew of tomatoes, herbs, olive oil and vinegar that usually features beef; *keftédes*, meat balls flavoured with herbs, usually coriander and cumin. Less common but well worth trying is *távas*, lamb or pork cooked in a clay pot with vegetables and spices. A variety of plain grilled steaks and chops also feature on all menus.

Vegetable dishes and accompaniments are scarce. In the tourist quarters, everything is served with French fries and either Greek or 'Village-style' salad, which are one and the same and contain lettuce or cabbage, cucumber, tomatoes, possibly olives and always a thick slice or two of *feta* cheese.

Meze

Meze, strictly speaking, are appetisers, though the *meze* which many restaurants in Cyprus offer indicates a full meal (in fact a meal and a half). A typical Cypriot *meze* consists of some 20-plus small dishes with a mixture of appetisers and small portions of main courses. It is an excellent crash course in Cypriot food and is usually good value, though invariably it must be ordered by a minimum of two people. The choice is usually meat *meze* or fish *meze*. Don't be afraid to ask what's in it. Keep in mind that although the portions are small, they do add up.

In more authentic restaurants, you should be able to get *louvia* (black-eyed beans) or *fasólia* (which may also be black-eyed beans or large white beans, usually served cold in a tomato and onion sauce), green beans or peas, tomatoes, courgettes and aubergine. Look out too for *kolokássia*, made from taro root, a relative of the yam.

Fish and Shellfish

As offshore catches get smaller and smaller, the choice of seafood becomes more limited and prices increase accordingly. Octopus *(chtapodi)* is often served in a red wine sauce. Prawns *(garídes)*, battered squid *(kalamari)* and spiny lobster are common menu items, but may be frozen, not fresh. This should be indicated on the menu but, if in doubt, ask.

Fresh fish that is generally available is swordfish *(xifías)*, red mullet *(barboúnia)*, red snapper *(sinagrida)*, gilt-head bream *(tsipoúra)* and sometimes whitebait *(marídes)*. Fish is usually simply barbecued. The speciality of the Troodos Mountains is farmed trout – smoked, sautéed or *au bleu* (poached with clarified butter).

Desserts and Sweets

Dessert usually means ice cream or fruit. Go for the latter. Depending on the season, you'll be able to try the island's outstanding honeydew and cantaloupe melons, watermelon, cherries, peaches, figs, apricots, oranges, bananas, tangerines, plums, grapes, pomegranates and more.

Cypriot sweets are rarely offered as dessert after a meal, but are sold separately in cafés or at specially set-up stalls. They are often very sweet. Honey and nuts are used in both *baklava*, a layered, strudel-like pastry, and *kataïfi*, a pastry that resembles shredded wheat. Another mouthwatering Cypriot speciality is *loukoumades*, a kind of sweet deep-fried doughnut dipped in syrup.

Coffee

Unless you specify Greek coffee, you will probably be served Nescafé – but not necessarily the brand itself, as this is the generic Greek term for instant coffee. In a DIY fashion, you are provided hot water with a sachet of instant powder. However, more places now offer filter coffee or cappuccino.

If you would prefer to try the local stuff, order *kafé elleniko* (Greek coffee), or simply *kahve* in the North. You will have to specify sweet *(gliko)*, medium-sweet *(metrio)*, or without sugar *(sketo)*. Greek coffee is taken black with a glass of

Oranges ready for picking

water. Try not to disturb or drink the thick grounds at the bottom of the cup.

Wines

Cypriot wines have been known and enjoyed since ancient times. Foremost among them is the sweet red Commandaria, originally produced for the Knights of St John at Kolossi. Celebrated as an apéritif or dessert wine, it is similar to Madeira and worth trying even if you don't normally like sweet wines. Sweet and dry wines of the sherry type are another speciality.

By northern European standards, the quality of Cypriot table wines is low, and a few are virtually undrinkable. It is always worth paying a little more and ordering a branded bottle; the majority are quite palatable, and a few are excellent. In a good restaurant the waiter will help you choose. Bella Pais, a rather bubbly white, makes a good apéritif or dessert wine. Duc de Nicosie is the closest a Cyprus wine comes to Champagne, and is produced using the traditional method.

Other Alcoholic Drinks

As an after-dinner drink, you may be offered a *zivania*, the local fire water. Distilled from the grape residue, it is similar to Greek *raki*. The other famous Greek drink enjoyed in Cyprus – though more by tourists than by the Cypriots – is *ouzo*, a clear aniseed-flavoured spirit that turns milky with the addition of water. (Confusingly, it is also called *raki* by the Turkish Cypriots).

Cypriot wines have been appreciated since antiquity

If you are going to drink Cypriot brandy straight, go for one of the better-known, more expensive brands, in order to avoid throat burn. A much more common use for local brandy is as the base for a brandy sour, the traditional island sundowner.

The local lagers (always referred to as beer), Keo and Leon are very good. Carlsberg is also brewed on the island.

TO HELP YOU ORDER...

Could we have a table?	**Tha boroúsame na échoume éna trapézi?**		
I'd like a/an/some...	**Tha íthela...**		
beer	**mía bíra**	milk	**gála**
bread	**psomí**	mineral water	**metallikó neró**
coffee	**éna kafé**	napkin	**petséta**
cutlery	**macheropírouna**	potatoes	**patátes**
dessert	**éna glikó**	rice	**rízi**
fish	**psári**	salad	**mía saláta**
fruit	**froúta**	soup	**mía soúpa**
glass	**éna potíri**	sugar	**záchari**
honey	**méli**	tea	**éna tsái**
ice cream	**éna pagotó**	wine	**krasí**
meat	**kréas**		

...AND READ THE MENU

afélia	pork stew	**loúnza**	smoked pork
barboúnia	red mullet	**marídes**	whitebait
fasólia	beans	**souvláki**	kebab
garídes	prawns	**stifádo**	stew (usually beef) with tomatoes
halloúmi	ewe's milk cheese		
keftédes	meatballs	**távas**	casserole in clay pot (usually lamb or pork)
kléftiko	roast lamb		
kolokássia	taro root ('Cypriot spinach')		
		tsipoúra	gilthead bream
koupépia	stuffed vine leaves	**xifías**	swordfish

PLACES TO EAT

We have used the following symbols to give an idea of the price for a three-course meal (or a meze) for one, excluding drinks:

€€€ over 40 euros   €€ 15–40 euros   € below 15 euros

SOUTHERN CYPRUS

NICOSIA

Arhondiko €€ *27 Odos Aristokyprou, Laiki Geitonia, tel: 2268 0080.* Open all day Monday to Saturday, and from 5pm on Sunday. This pretty little restaurant occupies a romantic setting with tables under the trees, in the heart of the restored, pedestrian Laiki Geitonia district. Try the traditional *meze*, stuffed vegetables, quail or pilaf, or push the boat out with gilthead sea bream.

Bonzai €€€ *Holiday Inn Nicosia, 70 Odos Rigainis, tel: 2271 2712.* Open daily for lunch and dinner. You can partake of Nicosia's more cosmopolitan character, when compared with the resorts, and take a break from Cypriot cuisine at this tolerably fine, if not quite rigorous Japanese restaurant inside the Holiday Inn, right next to the city walls. *Teppan yaki* and *sushi* dishes are served in a relaxed and friendly ambience.

Fifty-Nine Knives €€–€€€ *Classic Hotel, 94 Odos Rigainis, tel: 2266 4006.* Open daily for lunch and dinner (closed for dinner August). The name refers to an archaeological find below the present building, and this excellent little restaurant in a hotel next door to the Holiday Inn is a discovery in itself. Modern and stylish without being intimidating, it serves innovative Cypriot dishes with an international twist, as well as some interesting international dishes at reasonable prices.

Mattheos € *Plateia 28 Oktovriou, tel: 2275 5846.* Open Monday to Saturday noon–4pm. A no-frills locals' place, Matheos is recommended by everyone and is used to tourists. They serve all the usual favourites, but try something seasonal, such as quail or rabbit with pilaf. It's easy to find (at the back of the Faneromeni Church, beside the tiny mosque) and has outdoor and indoor seating.

LARNAKA

Art Cafe 1900 €€ *6 Odos Stasinou, tel: 2465 3027.* Open daily 6pm–midnight. Charming and arty, this café-restaurant is set in a lovely early 20th-century house opposite the Pierides Museum. Downstairs, among the artworks, drinks and snacks are served, while upstairs is an excellent, inventive restaurant. Home-cooked dishes include chicken in honey and lemon; chicken with orange juice, thyme and garlic; *távas* (traditional lamb or pork stew); stuffed vegetables and other vegetarian options. The café is run by a local radio celebrity and often on Friday evenings there is live music.

I Mavri Chelona €€ *11 Odos Mehmet Ali, tel: 2465 0661.* Open daily noon–midnight. Larnaka's old Turkish Quarter is home to some of the town's oldest and best restaurants, a description that does justice to 'The Black Turtle'. The upstairs dining room has old-fashioned charm to go along with smooth service and a menu that takes in some traditional home-cooking dishes.

Militzis €€ *42 Odos Piyale Paşa, tel: 2465 5867.* Open daily noon–midnight. Just south of the fort, Militzis has a windmill on its front terrace. A short meat-only menu features no-nonsense dishes such as *kokoretsi* (offal), *zalatina* (brawn/jellied pork), *kefalaki* (lamb's head) and more conventional grills and casseroles. *Kléftiko* (oven-roasted lamb) is a house speciality. Takeaway is available.

Varoshiotis Seafood Restaurant €€ *7 Odos Piyale Paşa, corner of Odos Sakarya, tel: 7000 3536.* Open daily for lunch and dinner. One of the best fish tavernas in town, it has been catering for locals as well as visitors since 1964. Try the fish *meze* – or just ask for whatever is fresh off the fishing boats that day.

AGIA NAPA AND REGION

Esperia €€ *46 Leoforos Archiepiskopou Makariou III, Agia Napa, tel: 2372 1635.* Open May–October daily 8am–midnight; November–April Monday to Friday 8am–5pm, Saturday and Sunday 8am–7pm. Seafood is the main fare at this restaurant right on the harbour (although the menu also has meat dishes). Ask for whatever is fresh off the fishing boats moored a few steps from your table, rather than be served with something imported and frozen. Accompanied by a village salad, a light Cypriot wine – and that harbour view – your meal should be memorable.

Limelight Taverna €€ *Odos Lipertis (opposite the post office), Agia Napa, tel: 2372 1650.* Open daily all day. A long-standing and reliable performer right in the heart of Agia Napa, this is the best grill house in town for steaks, but is also recommended for lamb, suckling pig and *souvláki*, all cooked over charcoal.

Potamos €€ *Limanaki, Potamos tou Liopetri, tel: 9963 5301.* Open Tuesday to Sunday, summer 10am–11pm, winter 10am–9pm. Taste is the unique selling point of this indelibly Cypriot seafood taverna, which is right beside the fishing boats at Potamos Creek. Few indeed are the concessions made either to sensitive foreign palates or twee restaurant design expectations. The food is authentic enough to be eaten by the fishermen who have just brought it ashore and the service is friendly but unornamented.

To Ploumin €€ *3 Odos Oktovriou 28, Sotira, tel: 2373 0444.* Usually open daily for lunch and dinner, but check in advance. This charming traditional taverna of formica-topped tables and Van Gogh-style wicker chairs was built in 1938 and is now a listed building. Signs around the village point the way. With displays of old tools, pottery, furniture and handicrafts, it is perfect for a home-cooked *meze*.

LIMASSOL (LEMESOS)

Blue Island €€ *3 Leoforos Amathoundos, tel: 2532 1466.* Open Monday to Saturday for dinner only. Classy and French-influenced, this restaurant on the old road to Nicosia offers a variety of international cuisines and seems equally at home with seafood, steaks and Cypriot dishes. The seafood *meze* is the speciality of the two brothers who own the place.

Karatello €€–€€€ *Odos Vasilissis 24, tel: 2582 0464.* Open daily for dinner. A renovated carob mill and warehouse from around 1900 close to the castle is the setting for this ultramodern and chic restaurant – an indicator of the direction in which the Cypriot dining scene is moving. The kitchen takes Cypriot and Greek stalwarts and serves them in updated form, with elements of fusion and other experimental styles.

The Ladas Old Harbour Fish Tavern €€–€€€ *Odos Saadi 1, Old Harbour, tel: 2536 5760.* Open Monday to Saturday for lunch and dinner. An atmospheric and friendly place at the old port that has been going strong for 50 years, and claims to be the oldest fresh fish taverna in Limassol. It is certainly one of the best, with an excellent selection of the best quality fish straight off the adjacent boats, usually simply grilled over charcoal. Popular with locals and visitors.

TROODOS MOUNTAINS

Linos Inn €€–€€€ *Old Kakopetria, tel: 2292 3161.* Open daily for lunch and dinner. A splendidly renovated taverna in an Alpine-looking setting of beautifully restored village houses *(see page 138)* in Old Kakopetria. Excellent, carefully prepared and inventive regional and Cypriot dishes.

The Mill €€–€€€ *8 Odos Mylou, Old Kakopetria, tel: 2292 2536.* Open daily for lunch and dinner. Set on the top floor of a hotel in a beautifully converted mill, this rambling and veteran restaurant is an experience in itself. Book a table on the small outside balcony if possible. The local speciality, fresh (farmed) trout, is almost *de rigueur* here, but the *souvláki* and *kléftiko* are also good.

Psilo Dhendro €€ *Platres–Troodos road, tel: 2542 1350.* Open daily 11am–5pm. A trout farm on the premises ensures that your choice of meal is just about decided for you at this popular and attractive establishment. A perfect place for rest and refreshment after walking the scenic trail to the Kalidonia waterfall *(see page 63)*, which starts and finishes here. Book before you set off.

PAFOS AND REGION

Cavallini €€€ *Leoforos Poseidonos (next to Amathus hotel), Kato Pafos, tel: 2696 4164.* Open Monday to Saturday from 7pm. Probably the best Italian restaurant in town, Cavallini offers sophisticated dining from a wide-ranging northern Italian menu, served in a stylish but cosy interior and on a lovely terrace that's unfortunately subjected to traffic noise.

Chez Alex/Stephanos €€€ *7 Odos Konstantia (corner of Odos Tefkrou), Kato Pafos, tel: 2693 4767.* Open daily for lunch and dinner. In a quiet part of the central nightlife area, this is among the town's best fish restaurants. If it swims, they cook it – give three hours' notice for their specials of Surprise Sea Bream (baked in a salt crust) or *bouillabaisse*; 12 hours' notice for lobster. Dining room with terrace.

Demokritos €€ *1 Odos Dionysou, Kato Pafos, tel: 2693 3371.* Open nightly. It's hard to miss Demokritos – just follow the crowds, who later sit wide-eyed at the glass-balancing acts of its staff. Open since 1971, it is the oldest taverna-restaurant in Pafos. It trades more heavily on its music and dancing than its food, which is inevitably compromised due to numbers. But it's still a good night out.

Kiniras €€ *91 Leoforos Archiepiskopou Makariou III, Ktima (Upper Pafos), tel: 2694 1604.* Open daily for lunch and dinner, or for drinks at any time. The garden courtyard of the Kiniras hotel *(see page 140)* is one of the nicest places to eat in Pafos. The food is excellent and portions are hearty. The menu features some inventive international dishes, but ask the proprietor, George, for his recommendation and you will probably be steered towards a traditional favourite such as *kléftiko* or *stifado*.

Pelican €€ *102 Leoforos Apostolos Pavlou, The Harbour, Kato Pafos, tel: 2695 2500.* Open daily all day. Occupying a smart terrace on the harbourfront, the Pelican is probably the best of several unspectacular tavernas that compete for customers here, in a setting that's so scenic that tables are always in demand. Go for a fish *meze* or a swordfish special.

Peyia Tavern €€ *Leoforos Kyprianou, Pegeia, tel: 2662 1077.* Open daily for dinner. Pegeia, a burgeoning village north of Pafos, just inland from Coral Bay, has long had a cluster of fine traditional tavernas on and around its main square. This one serves up no-frills home cooking in a plain old-fashioned setting, or on the tiny terrace out front, and fills up quickly every evening.

Seacrest €€–€€€ *Lakki Harbour, tel: 2632 1333.* Open daily all day. You probably won't go wrong at any of Lakki's harbourside restaurants, as they all serve fish straight from the boat to the oven. Seacrest is one of the best, with a perfect harbour view. Splurge on the Seacrest Special – lobster stuffed with sole and crabmeat.

Seven St George's Tavern €€ *Odos Pavlou Krinaiou, Geros kipou, just off the main road to Kato Pafos, tel: 2696 3176.* Open Tuesday to Sunday for lunch and dinner. It's not easy to find this charming garden taverna, but it is well worth the effort. George and Lara, the affable owners, offer what could well be the best *meze* on the island (including a vegetarian option). The quality of the food, the range of dishes, the service and the atmosphere are light years away from the anonymous *moussaka*-and-chips joints of Kato Pafos.

Ta Bania €€ *Leoforos Poseidonos, Kato Pafos, tel: 2694 1558.* Open daily all day. Set right on the seafront in a busy part of town, Ta Bania means 'the baths', referring to the municipal swimming pool immediately next door. It's a popular, friendly and enjoyable place to catch the breeze, and is surprisingly sheltered from the hubbub. The atmosphere is that of a bright, blue-and-white Mediterranean seaside café. A wide range of snacks and full meals is on offer, though the quality of the latter is variable.

NORTHERN CYPRUS

NORTHERN NICOSIA (LEFKOŞA)

Saray Roof €€ *In the Saray Hotel, Atatürk Meydanı, tel: 228 3115.* It would be more accurate to say 'on the Saray Hotel'. A superb rooftop location with an unbeatable view over the city is this restaurant's unique selling point. The Turkish and Continental dishes on the menu are polished enough, but don't quite reach the heights.

KERYNEIA (GIRNE)

Canlı Balık € *Kordonboyou, tel: 815 2182.* Probably the best of the many fish restaurants in at the splendid Keryneia harbour, Canlı Balık enjoys an elevated centre-stage view of one of the island's most scenic settings and serves consistently good fish dishes. Ideal for lunch.

Saint-Tropez €€ *Karaoğlanoğlu Caddesi, Karavas (Alsancak), tel: 821 8324.* Open for lunch and dinner, Monday to Saturday in summer and Tuesday to Sunday in winter. The mini Eiffel Tower in the garden is not entirely appropriate for the real Saint-Tropez perhaps, but for a French restaurant it's close enough. Authentic French cuisine served in elegant surroundings means tables at this family-run establishment on the Keryneia–Lapithos (Girne–Lapta) road are often in demand. Specialities include *crêpes Suzette* flamed at your table.

FAMAGUSTA (GAZIMAĞUSA)

La Veranda € *Nemık Kemal Meydanı, tel: 367 0153.* Plain, wholesome Turkish fare that doesn't extend much beyond kebabs and salads – but good ones – keeps the customers satisfied on the outdoor terrace in the city's main square, with a romantic view of the Lala Mustafa Paşa Mosque and the Venetian governor's palace.

A–Z TRAVEL TIPS

A Summary of Practical Information

A

ACCOMMODATION (see also CAMPING, YOUTH HOSTELS, and RECOM-
MENDED HOTELS on pages 135–41)

For the high season (mid-June to October), try to book well in
advance in order to get the place of your choice. The Cyprus
Tourism Organisation *(see pages 131–2)* produces a brochure listing virtually all hotels and many other types of accommodation.
If you arrive without a booking, contact the CTO at the airport
or in Nicosia, Larnaka, Limassol, Pafos, Agia Napa, Polis or Pano
Platres for advice.

Hotels. Cyprus has hotels in all categories, from five-star luxury
havens and comfortable guest-houses to pleasant apartment-hotels
(classified A, B, C and Tourist Apartments). All hotels offer dis-
counts during the low season, which for seaside resorts is from 16
November to 15 March, and for hill resorts from 1 October to 30
June – both excluding the Christmas/New Year and Easter holiday
periods. Some resort hotels close during the low season.

Villas. Self-contained villas may be rented through local agencies,
or you can inquire at the CTO. Unlike on the small Greek islands,
accommodation in unregistered private houses is not available.

Agrotourism. Thanks to an initiative by the CTO, some traditional
houses in the countryside have been renovated and are now rented
out as holiday homes. For details, ask the CTO for a brochure or
contact the Cyprus Agrotourism Company, 19 Leoforos Lemesou,
PO Box 24535, 1390 Nicosia, Cyprus; tel: 2234 0071; www.agro
tourism.com.cy.

I'd like a single/double room	**Tha íthela éna monó/dipló domátio**
with bath/shower	**me bánio/dous**
What's the rate per night?	**Piá íne i timí giá mía níkta?**

AIRPORTS

Larnaka International Airport (LCA; tel: 2481 6400; www.cyprus airports.com.cy), the principal air gateway to Cyprus, lies 5km (3 miles) from Larnaka town and 50km (30 miles) from Nicosia. Buses run frequently between the airport and Larnaka, Limassol, Nicosia, Agia Napa and Protaras. Daytime taxi fares range from €10 to the centre of Larnaka up to €100 to Pafos. A few local buses operate daily to Larnaka.

Pafos International Airport (PFO; tel: 2481 6400; www.cyprus airports.com.cy), 11km (7 miles) southeast of Pafos on the west coast, handles some scheduled and many charter services, which helps to ease congestion at Larnaka. Buses run frequently between the airport and Pafos and Limassol. Daytime taxi fares range from €30 to the centre of Pafos up to €60 to Limassol.

Ercan International Airport (ECN; tel: 231 4806; www.cypnet. co.uk) in Northern Cyprus, 14km (9 miles) east of Nicosia, is served by flights from Turkey only. There is no airport bus service. Taxis serve all points in the North.

B

BICYCLE AND MOTORCYCLE HIRE

You can hire bikes and motorcycles in all important towns and re-sorts. To operate a motorcycle or motor scooter, you must be at least 18 years of age and hold a driver's licence (17-year-olds may hire a moped of 49cc). It is illegal not to wear a crash helmet and the police are more likely to enforce this regulation these days. Moped hire is cheap (about €10 per day), but check your holiday insurance covers you.

Mountain biking, particularly in the Troodos Mountains and Pen-tadaktylos (Beşparmak) Mountains, and on the Akamas Peninsula, is popular but strenuous, so be sure you are up to the challenge before setting out. Cycling along the coast is far easier. The CTO *(see pages 131–2)* has a brochure, *Cyprus for Cycling*, detailing 19 routes in the South. For more details, contact the Cyprus Cycling Federation; tel: 2244 9870, www.cypruscycling.com.

BUDGETING FOR YOUR TRIP

Pricewise, Cyprus is above average as a Mediterranean destination – more expensive than most Greek islands, Turkey and parts of Spain and southern Portugal, but cheaper than much of mainland Europe. In high season, airfares from Britain cost around £200–300 and a good four-star hotel's room rate is around €150 per night. Booking a package, particularly at the last minute, will save you money.

Food and drink is moderate (a three-course meal plus drinks in a simple restaurant usually comes to around €25 per person). Drinks in bars and restaurants range from €2 for a beer in a simple place to €10 and over for cocktails in a fancy establishment. Museum entry is generally inexpensive, ranging from under a euro to about €5.

C

CAMPING

Campsites in the South are licensed by the Cyprus Tourism Organisation. They provide electricity, toilets, showers, a food shop and a café. There are five official sites: Troodos; Polis; Governor's Beach, near Limassol; Geroskipou, near Pafos; and Feggari/Coral Bay, near Pafos. Ask at the nearest CTO office *(see page 132)*.

| Is there a campsite nearby? | **Ipárchi éna méros giá kataskínosi/'camping' edó kondá?** |

CAR HIRE *(see also DRIVING)*

As many sights in Cyprus are spread out, and beyond the reach of public transport, it is worth hiring a car.

Reserve a car in advance – especially for the high season. To hire a car, you must have a valid national driver's licence (held for at least three years) or an International Driving Permit. Depending on the company, the minimum age is 21 to 25. Drivers under 25 pay an insurance premium. A deposit is usually required, payable by credit card. Check whether driving on unsurfaced roads will invalidate the insurance, and on the position with taking the car into the North.

Budget (tel: 2482 2666, www.budgetcyprus.com), Thrifty (tel: 2532 1271, www.thrifty.com.cy), Hertz (tel: 2220 8888, www.hertz.com.cy), Avis (tel: 2271 3333, www.avis.com.cy) and Europcar (tel: 2464 3085, www.europcar.com.cy) all have offices in the major cities in the South, and representatives at Larnaka and Pafos airports and at the main resorts.

Cypriot firms like Petsas (tel: 2245 6450, www.petsas.com.cy) generally charge less than international firms and some of them provide equally good cars and service.

Rates are cheap (from around €30 per day), though you will have to add another €10 or so for Collision Damage Waiver insurance, and perhaps another €2 to cover damage to the tyres or windscreen. For a decent family-sized car, plan on spending up to €50 per day. In summer, air-conditioning is essential. Note that the rate always includes unlimited mileage.

I'd like to hire a car (tomorrow) for one day/a week Please include full insurance.	**Tha íthela na nikiáso éna aftokínito (ávrio) giá mía iméra/mía evdomáda Sas parakaló na simberilávete plíri asfália.**

CLIMATE

Cyprus enjoys sunny skies and low humidity almost all year round. On the coast, sea breezes temper the 32°C (90°F) heat of July and August, but in Nicosia you can add on 4 or 5 degrees, and the thermometer often goes above 38°C (100°F).

January and February see snowfalls in the Troodos mountain range – most years there is enough to allow some skiing. It rains occasionally between October and February, but there is plenty of sunshine, too, and the sea temperature remains just about warm enough for swimming.

The following are average coastal temperatures:

	J	F	M	A	M	J	J	A	S	O	N	D
max °C	17	17	19	23	26	30	32	33	31	27	22	18
°F	63	63	66	73	79	86	90	91	88	81	72	64
min °C	8	8	9	12	16	19	21	21	20	16	12	9
°F	46	46	48	54	61	66	70	70	68	61	54	48

CLOTHING

In summer, wear comfortable, loose cotton clothing. July and August nights are very warm, but at other times of the year, they can be cool (so can air-conditioned rooms), so a light sweater is a good idea. In winter (late November to March), you'll need a raincoat or light winter coat, a warm sweater or jacket, and warmer clothes.

On the beach, toplessness is widely tolerated; however, nudity in public is unacceptable. Informality is the general rule, but in the more posh hotels and restaurants, people often dress up in the evening (and may be required to do so).

Men will need to wear long trousers to visit Orthodox monasteries and women must wear a long skirt (often provided) and a modest top.

CRIME AND SAFETY

There is still so little crime on Cyprus that the few robberies which do take place make headlines, but crime rates are rising. The island's only violence generally occurs in drunken brawls in Agia Napa and other busy tourist centres. Take the same precautions as you would at home.

D

DRIVING

Road conditions. Driving conditions are generally good in Cyprus, with well-surfaced, well-marked roads and fast motorways running along the south coast, linking Limassol, Larnaka, Agia Napa and Pafos, and heading inland to Nicosia. Beware of speeding on these roads as there are frequent police patrols.

Most of the main roads are paved and in good condition, and even many of the secondary roads are easily negotiated. Short dis-

Are we on the right road for ...?	**Ímaste sto drómo giá ...?**
left/right	**aristerá/dexiá**
up/down	**epáno/káto**
Full tank, please.	**Na to gemísete me venzíni.**
normal/super/lead-free	**aplí/soúper/amólivdos**
My car has broken down.	**Épatha mía vlávi.**
There's been an accident.	**Égine éna disteíchima.**
(international) driving permit	**(diethnís) ádia odigíseos**
car registration papers	**ádia kikloforías**
collision insurance	**asfália enandíon trítou**
Check the oil/tyres/battery.	**Na eléchsete ta ládia/ta lá ticha/ti bataría.**

tances on minor roads, typically in the hills, can often be tackled in an ordinary car, but they are often unpaved and pock-marked with potholes in addition to having steep, hairpin turns. You should be alert at all times on these roads. A four-wheel-drive vehicle is best for this kind of driving. There are many rough tracks, which may invalidate your hire-car insurance.

In the cities traffic is fairly orderly. During the rush hour, you can expect to encounter traffic jams in Nicosia, Larnaka, Limassol and Pafos.

Rules and regulations. British and Irish motorists will feel at home in Cyprus, where traffic keeps to the left. Seat-belt use is compulsory in the front of cars and, where fitted, in the back, too. Always carry your driving licence and car-hire documents with you.

Speed limits. The speed limits are 50kph (30mph) in town and 100kph (60mph) on highways (lower limits may be posted).

Fuel. The price of fuel in Cyprus compares with elsewhere in Europe. Diesel fuel is cheaper than petrol, and it is possible to hire diesel cars. Filling stations generally close on Sundays and public holidays, but many have self-service fuel pumps that take cash or credit cards. They are plentiful in and around the main towns and resorts, but are scarcer in the mountains. If you're setting out on a mountain excursion, make sure the tank is full.

Parking. This can be a problem in Nicosia, Limassol, Pafos, Agia Napa and Larnaka. Fines are given for illegal parking. Try to find a meter or car park.

Problems. Call your hire company first, then try the Cyprus Automobile Association; tel: 2231 3131 (24-hour assistance). In an emergency, call the police, tel: 112 (in the North 155).

Road signs. Most road signs, and most other signs imparting general information, are the standard pictographs used throughout Europe, and all the written signs are in both English and Greek (in the North the signs are in Turkish and English).

E

ELECTRICITY

The standard current is 240 volts, 50 Hz AC; sockets are usually three-pin, as in the UK. Adapters are available in hotels and shops. Most hotels and some apartments have 110-volt outlets for razors.

| I need an adapter/ battery, please. | **Chriázome éna metaschimatistí/ mia bataría, parakaló.** |

EMBASSIES AND CONSULATES

The following embassies and consulates are all in Nicosia:

Australia: High Commission, 4 Odos Annis Komninis; tel: 2275 3001, www.cyprus.embassy.gov.au

Canada: Consulate, 1 Odos Lampousas; tel: 2277 5508

Ireland: Embassy, 7 Odos Aiantas; tel: 2281 8183, www.embassy ofireland.com.cy

UK: High Commission, Odos Alexandrou Palli; tel: 2286 1100, http://ukincyprus.fco.gov.uk/en

US: Embassy, Corner of Odos Metochiou and Odos Ploutarchou, Egkomi; tel: 2239 3939, http://nicosia.usembassy.gov

EMERGENCIES

Republic of Cyprus:
Police, ambulance and fire brigade: **112**

Northern Cyprus:
Police: **155**; ambulance: **112**; fire brigade: **199**

| careful | **prosochí** | police | **astinomía** |
| help | **voíthia** | stop | **stamatíste** |

G

GAY AND LESBIAN TRAVELLERS

Southern Cyprus has a small but growing gay and lesbian scene, and a slowly improving acceptance of both the local gay and lesbian community and visitors from off-island. Gay Cyprus (www.gay-cyprus.com) has details on the community and the scene. Other useful sources of information include www.gaycyprus.org and www.cyprusgayforum.com.

Northern Cyprus is considerably more conservative. Turkeygay.net has a page of information on Northern Cyprus (www.turkeygay.net/cyprus.html).

GETTING THERE (see also AIRPORTS)

For most people, air travel is the only practical way of getting to Cyprus. Direct scheduled and charter flights link several British airports to Larnaka and Pafos. The flying time is around 4 hours 30 minutes. In addition to the many chartered airlines that fly to Cyprus, important carriers with direct services from the UK include **Cyprus Airways** (www.cyprusair.com.cy) and **British Airways** (www.britishairways.com).

There are no non-stop flights from North America, but connecting services operate to Larnaka from major cities. Most Australian travellers to Cyprus fly by way of Athens, Istanbul or London.

Turkish and Turkish Cypriot airlines, both charter and scheduled, fly to Northern Cyprus from abroad via an intermediate stop in Turkey.

GUIDES AND TOURS

There are various guided coach tours that cover such places as Kykkos Monastery and the Troodos Mountains, Pafos, Nicosia and Kourion. Some of the most interesting tours on the island are run by a company called Exalt (short for Excursion Alternatives; tel:

2531 5154), who specialise in off-the-beaten-track jeep and trekking expeditions, devoted to environmentally-friendly exploration of the Cypriot wilderness. Their principal geographical area of expertise is the Akamas Peninsula and the Pafos Forest region, but they also cover parts of the Troodos Mountains.

Taxi drivers can be hired for half-day or full-day tours. Most drivers speak English, and are willing to negotiate a fare for tours.

H

HEALTH AND MEDICAL CARE (see also EMERGENCIES)

Medical treatment and assistance is offered free of charge to tourists in case of emergency, but to be completely at ease, it is recommended that you take out travel insurance to cover any risk of illness and accident while on holiday. Visitors from Britain, Ireland and other European countries should take with them a European Health Insurance card (EHIC), which allows for free or reduced-cost medical treatment.

There are very capable doctors and dentists in the resorts, cities and larger towns, as well as good hospital facilities. Your hotel will advise you of the nearest doctor and most of them speak English. Doctors on call at weekends are listed in local newspapers or can

Where's the nearest (all-night) pharmacy?	**Pou íne to kondinótero (dianikterévon) farmakío?**
I need a doctor/dentist	**Chriázome éna giatró/odontogiatró**
an ambulance	**éna asthenofóro**
a hospital	**nosokomío**
I have...	**Écho...**
a headache	**ponokéfalo**
a fever	**piretós**
an upset stomach	**pónos stí kiliá**

be contacted as follows: Nicosia, tel: 9090 1422; Agia Napa, tel: 9090 1423; Larnaka, tel: 9090 1424; Limassol, tel: 9090 1425; Pafos, tel: 9090 1426.

Stomach upsets should not be a problem, as hotels and restaurants observe high standards of cleanliness. Tap water is safe to drink. The

A	α	a	as in bar
B	β	v	
Γ	γ	g	as in 'go' (before i- and e- sounds, pronounce like y in 'yes')
Δ	δ	d	like th in 'this'
E	ε	e	as in 'get'
Z	ζ	z	
H	η	i	like ee in 'meet'
Θ	θ	th	as in 'thin'
I	ι	i l	ike ee in 'meet'
K	κ	k	
Λ	λ	l	
M	μ	m	
N	ν	n	
Ξ	ξ	x	like ks in 'thanks'
O	ο	o	as in 'got'
Π	π	p	
P	ρ	r	
Σ	σ, ς	s	as in 'kiss'
T	τ	t	
Y	υ	i	like ee in 'meet'
Φ	φ	f	
X	χ	ch	as in Scottish 'loch'
Ψ	ψ	ps	as in tipsy
O/Ω	ω	o	as in 'got'
OY	ου	oo	as in 'soup'

sun can bronze you, but also burn you. Take it in very small doses at first and use sunscreen, particularly if you have delicate skin.

Pharmacies (ΦAPMAKEIO – *farmakío*) are recognised by the sign outside – a red cross on a white background. They are open Monday–Friday 7.30 or 8am–1pm and 3 or 4–7pm (mornings only on Wednesday and Saturday). Certain pharmacies offer a 24-hour service – see local papers for listings.

Most medicines sold in the UK, US, Canada and Europe are available, but often require a prescription. Pharmacists can generally advise on minor problems such as cuts, sunburn, blisters and gastric disorders.

L

LANGUAGE

English is spoken almost as a dual language in all the resorts, and is understood by many people in Cyprus, both North and South. It is only well off the beaten track that a familiarity with Greek (in Southern Cyprus) or Turkish (in Northern Cyprus) is useful. If you do speak Greek, be aware that Cypriot Greek can be very different from that spoken in Greece. There is a distinctive accent (often incomprehensible to other Greeks), and about 15 percent of the vocabulary is unique to the island.

The table on the left lists the Greek alphabet with their capital and small forms, followed by the letter to which they correspond in English. Below are a few phrases you might want to use:

hello	**yásoo (informal), yásas (formal)**
good morning	**kaliméra**
good afternoon/evening	**kalispéra**
good night	**kaliníkta**
goodbye	**chérete**

please	**parakaló**
thank you	**efcharistó**
yes	**ne**
no	**óchi**
I don't speak Greek.	**Den miló elliniká.**
Do you speak English?	**Miláte angliká?**
excuse me	**me sinchoríte**
you're welcome	**parakaló**
where/when/how	**pou/póte/pos**
how long/how far	**póso keró/póso makriá**
yesterday/today/tomorrow	**chthes/símera/ávrio**
day/week/month/year	**iméra/evdomáda/mínas/chrónos**
left/right	**aristerá/dexiá**
up/down	**epáno/káto**
good/bad	**kalós/kakós**
big/small	**megálos/mikrós**
cheap/expensive	**ftinós/akrivós**
open/closed	**aniktós/klistós**
here/there	**edó/ekí**
free (vacant)/occupied	**eléftheri/kratiméni**
early/late	**norís/argá**
easy/difficult	**éfkolos/dískolos**
What does this mean?	**Ti siméni aftó?**
I don't understand.	**Den katalavéno.**
Please write it down.	**Parakaló grápste to.**
Is there an admission charge?	**Prépi na pliróso ísodo?**
Waiter, please!	**Garsóni (garçon), parakaló!**
I'd like...	**Tha íthela...**
How much is that?	**Póso káni aftó?**
Have you something less expensive?	**Échete káti ftinótero?**
What time is it?	**Ti óra íne?**

M

MAPS

The Cyprus Tourism Organisation provides a comprehensive island map and town plans of Nicosia, Limassol, Larnaka, Pafos, Agia Napa and Protaras, and their environs, plus the Troodos Mountains, free of charge to visitors.

| I'd like a street plan of... | **Tha íthela éna odikó chárti tis...** |
| a road map of this region | **éna chárti aftís tis periochís** |

MEDIA

Newspapers and magazines. There is a good selection of British and Irish newspapers and major American weekly news magazines available. Foreign newspapers generally arrive a day after publication. The *Cyprus Mail*, an English-language daily, has current news coverage and a good What's On section and weekly review magazine. The *Cyprus Weekly* (also in English) carries lively features and helpful information. Most resorts have some sort of free What's On magazine that can be picked up at the tourist office, hotels, restaurants, bars and nightspots. In the North there's *Cyprus Today*, a weekly newspaper in English.

| Have you any English- | **Échete anglikés** |
| language newspapers? | **efimerídes?** |

Radio and TV. The Cyprus Broadcasting Corporation (CyBC) transmits English-language programmes on FM 91.1, 92.4, 94.2 and 96.5 with a bulletin at 10am. News and features are broadcast 1.30–3pm and 7–8pm (depending upon the season) until midnight. The BBC World Service and Radio BFBS (British Forces Broadcasting

Service) are on the air 24 hours a day. Some hotels have BBC Radio Five Live. Nearly all hotels with three or more stars offer cable and satellite television channels, including BBC World News, CNN and Sky. British football matches and other popular sporting events can be watched on television in bars that subscribe to Sky Sports and/or the BBC.

MONEY *(see also OPENING HOURS)*

Currency. The euro is the national currency of Southern Cyprus. Cypriot euro coins have images of the indigenous moufflon wild sheep (1, 2 and 5 cents), the ancient Kyrenia ship (10, 20 and 50 cents), and the prehistoric idol of Pomos (€1 and €2). The euro banknotes are €5, €10, €20, €50, €100, €200 and €500.

In Northern Cyprus, the New Turkish lira (YTL) is the local currency. However, euros, pounds and dollars are usually accepted in hotels, restaurants and other businesses.

Currency exchange. Hotels can change money and traveller's cheques, but you will tend to get much better rates at a bank (ΤΡΑΠΕΖΑ, *trápeza*).

Traveller's cheques. Traveller's cheques are widely accepted, but are best cashed at a bank.

Credit cards. Major credit cards are welcome as payment in most city shops, hotels and many, but by no means all, restaurants, as well as by all the international and local car-hire firms. Take along your passport to use as identification.

I want to change some pounds/dollars.	**Thélo n alláxo merikés líres/ meriká dollária.**
Do you accept traveller's cheques?	**Pérnete traveller's cheques?**
Can I pay with this credit card?	**Boró na pliróso me aftí ti pistotikí kárta?**

O

OPENING HOURS

National museums and archaeological sites. Open all year Monday–Saturday 9am–5pm, Sunday 10am–1pm. Other museums keep similar but usually shorter hours, and may be closed on Saturday afternoon and all day Sunday (see Where to Go chapter for individual museums).

Banks. Monday–Friday 8.15am–12.30pm during July and August. At other times of year, Monday–Friday 8.30am–12.30pm, and 3.15–4.45pm on Monday only. Some banks in tourist centres reopen, for currency exchange only, 4–7pm (summer) and 3–6pm (winter).

Shops. In summer, spring and autumn, the siesta is still observed by many shops. Most are open Monday–Saturday 8am–1pm and 4–7pm (closing half an hour earlier or later depending upon season). There is no afternoon reopening on Wednesday and Saturday year-round. From October to April, there is no siesta; closing time is around 6pm.

P

POLICE

Police emergency numbers:
In the South: **112**
In the North: **155**

The police headquarters in Nicosia are at Leoforos Strovolou, and there are divisional offices and stations in all of the main towns and resorts. Regular police officers in Southern Cyprus wear blue uniforms and they cruise around in blue-and-white police cars. Most

| Where's the nearest police station? | Pou íne to kondinótero astinomikó tmíma? |

members of the police (*Astynomía* in Greek; *Polis* in Turkish) speak some English. You'll recognise the traffic policemen by their white gloves and sleeves.

POST OFFICES

District Post Offices, of which there are two in both Nicosia and Limassol, and one in both Larnaka and Pafos, are open Mon–Fri 7.30am–1.30pm and 3–6pm (4–7pm in July and Aug; closed Wednesday afternoons all year) and Sat 8.30–10.30am. All other post offices are open Mon–Fri 7.30am–1.30pm, plus Thur 3–6pm (closed Thursday afternoons in July and Aug). Postboxes are coloured yellow in both the South and North.

Postage stamps may be bought at hotels, newsstands and kiosks. Postcards to Europe arrive within a week.

Where's the (nearest) post office/telephone office?	**Pou íne to kodinótero tachidromío/cyta?**
A stamp for this letter/ postcard, please.	**Éna grammató simo giaftó to grámma/graftí tin kárta, parakaló.**
express/registered	**exprés/sistiméno**
airmail	**aeroporikós**

PUBLIC HOLIDAYS

In addition to their own national holidays, Cypriots also celebrate certain Greek or Turkish holidays. Offices close on the following days. Shops remain open on some holidays: ask locally as to which ones.

1 Jan	*Protochroniá*	New Year's Day
6 Jan	*ton Theofaníon*	Epiphany
25 Mar	*Ikostí Pémti Martíou (tou Evangelismoú)*	Greek Independence Day

I Apr	*Iméra enárxeos kipriakoú*	Greek Cypriot National Day
I May	*Protomagiá*	Labour Day
15 Aug	*Dekapentávgoustos (tis Panagías)*	Assumption Day
I Oct	*Iméra tis anexartisías (tis Kíprou)*	Cyprus Independence Day
28 Oct	*Ikostí Ogdói Oktovríou ('Ochi')*	'No' Day, commemorating Greek defiance of Italian invasion of 1940
24/25 Dec	*Christoúgenna*	Christmas Eve/Day
26 Dec	*Défteri Iméra ton Christougénnon*	St Stephen's Day

Movable dates:

Katharí Deftéra	1st Day of Lent/Ash Monday (also known as Green Monday)
Megáli Paraskeví	Good Friday
Deftéra tou Páscha	Easter Monday
Kataklyzmós	Pentecost (Festival of the Flood)

Are you open tomorrow?   **Iste aniktí ávrio?**

R

RELIGION

It is important that you dress modestly when visiting churches, monasteries and mosques. The dress code for monasteries is usually rigidly enforced and specifies long trousers for men, a calf-length or longer skirt for women and covered shoulders for both sexes. Churches are generally less formal. You must remove your shoes before entering a mosque.

T

TELEPHONE

To call Southern Cyprus from abroad, the international dialling code is 357; for the North it is 90392. To make international calls from Cyprus, dial 00 for an international connection, then the country code. For directory enquiries in Cyprus dial 192.

Public telephones can be used for local and international calls. All have instructions in English. A phone card, available in a selection of prices, is the simplest way to make an international call.

In most hotels, you can dial long-distance from your room, but the charges are high. Standard rates and other information are available from long-distance operators, all of whom speak English (tel: 194).

Area codes do not exist in Cyprus. Instead, there are eight-digit numbers in the South. In Nicosia, they start with 22; Agia Napa 23; Larnaka 24; Limassol 25; Pafos 26. In the North, numbers consist of seven digits, and localities can be determined by the first three.

TIME ZONES

The chart on the next page shows the time differences between Cyprus, which is on Eastern European Time (EET), and various cities in winter (UTC/GMT + 2 hours). In summer, clocks are put forward 1 hour, so the time difference with the UK and US stays the same.

New York	London	**Cyprus**	Jo'burg	Sydney	Auckland
5am	10am	**noon**	noon	9pm	11pm

TIPPING

Service charges are included in hotel, restaurant and taverna bills, but a little extra is always appreciated, especially for good service.

Average tips:

Hotel porter, per bag	€2
Maid, per day	€2
Waiter/barman	15 percent
Taxi driver	10 percent
Tour guide (private)	around 10 percent
Tour guide (group tour)	from €2 per day
Hair stylist/barber	10 percent

TOILETS

Public toilets exist in larger towns, but not in great numbers. Museums often have the cleanest facilities, and the ones on the government-run 'tourist beaches' are excellent. Generally standards are reasonable. Toilets are usually indicated in both English and Greek.

Where are the toilets?   **Pou íne ta apohoritíra?**

TOURIST INFORMATION

The **Cyprus Tourism Organisation**, or CTO *(Kypriakós Organismós Tourismoú – KOT)*, which covers the South, is a mine of information, with free brochures and maps. The staff are knowledgeable and helpful.

UK: 17 Hanover Street, London, W1S 1YP; tel: (020) 7569 8800; fax: (020) 7499 4935; email: informationcto@btconnect.com; www.visitcyprus.com

US: 13 E 40th Street, New York, NY 10016; tel: (212) 683 5280; fax: (212) 683 5282; email: gocyprus@aol.com; www.visitcyprus.com

For information on **Northern Cyprus**:

UK: 29 Bedford Square, London, WC1B 3EO; tel: (020) 7631 1930; fax: (020) 7462 9789; email: info@go-northcyprus.com; www.e-kktc.com

US: 1667 K Street, Suite 690, Washington DC, 20006; tel: (202) 887 6198; fax: (202) 467 0685; email: trncdc@verizon.com; www. trncwashdc.org

The CTO's head office in Nicosia (not open to the public) is at 19 Leoforos Lemesou, PO Box 24535, 1390 Lefkosia; tel: 2269 1100; fax: 2233 1644; email: cytour@visitcyprus.com; www.visit cyprus.com. The CTO maintains offices at **Larnaka airport** (tel: 2464 3576); at **Pafos Airport** (tel: 2642 3161); at **Limassol harbour** (to meet ferries and cruise ships; tel: 2557 1868); and in the major tourist centres:

Nicosia: 11 Odos Aristokyprou, Laiki Geitonia; tel: 2267 4264.

Limassol: 115a Odos Spyrou Araouzou; tel: 2536 2756; 22 Odos Georgiou A', Potamos tis Germasogeias; tel: 2532 3211.

Larnaka: Plateia Vasileos Pavlou; tel: 2465 4322.

Pafos: 3 Odos Gladstonos, Ktima; tel: 2693 2841. 63a Leoforos Poseidonos, Kato Pafos; tel: 2693 0521.

Agia Napa: 12 Leoforos Kryou Nerou; tel: 2372 1796.

Polis: 2 Odos Vasileos Stasioikou A'; tel: 2632 2468.

Pano Platres: Plateia; tel: 2542 1316. (For the Troodos area visit this office.)

Paralimni/Protaras: 356 Leoforos Protara-Kavo Gkreko, Paralimni; tel: 2383 2865.

In Northern Cyprus, tourist information is available from the Ministry of Tourism, Lefkoşa, Turkish Republic of Northern Cyprus, c/o Mersin-10, Turkey; tel: 228 9629; fax: 227 3976.

In addition, there are tourist offices in **Keryneia/Girne** (30 Kordonboyu Sokagı – the harbour; tel: 815 2145); **Famagusta/ Gazimağusa** (Akkule (White Bastion), Land Gate, Venetian Walls; tel: 366 2864); and **Nicosia/Lefkoşa** (at the Keryneia/Girne Gate; tel: 228 8765).

Where's the tourist office?   **Pou íne to grafío tourismoú?**

TRANSPORT

Cyprus has no railways and the inter-urban bus service is not always frequent, especially on Sundays. Bus services in the towns and resorts, however, are good, but service to and from villages – if it exists at all – is just one or two buses per day. Private and shared taxis fill the public transport gap.

Private taxis. Vehicles are metered. You can hail a taxi on the street or call for one by telephone. The numbers of the various private companies are listed in the local telephone directory.

Shared service taxis and minibuses. In the South, service taxis take from four to eight passengers and connect all major towns every half-hour. Ask the tourist office for a schedule *(see page 132)*. Prices are fixed and very reasonable, so this is a good way to get from one town to another on a budget. In the North, minibuses called *dolmuş* operate between the towns but only depart when they are full.

Where can I get a taxi/ shared taxi/ minibus?	**Pou boró na vro éna taxí/ epivatikó taxí/ mikro poúlman?**
May I have a place in this taxi for…?	**Thélo mía thési sto taxí giá…?**
What's the fare to…?	**Piá íne i timí giá…?**

V

VISAS AND ENTRY REQUIREMENTS

Entering the Republic. Nationals of the EU, Australia, Canada, Japan, New Zealand, Singapore, the US and some other countries can stay in Cyprus for up to three months without a visa. Legal points of entry are the ports of Larnaka, Limassol and Pafos, and the international airports of Larnaka and Pafos.

Entering the North. Visitors travelling via Ercan airport or the ports of Famagusta (Gazimağusa), Keryneia (Girne) or Karavostasi (Gemikonaği) in Turkish-controlled Northern Cyprus, and who are citizens of countries that do not require a visa to enter Cyprus, may cross freely in both directions between North and South at the official crossing points. But if they are resident in the North for 90 days or more, they may require a residency permit issued by the authorities in the South to be able to cross without hindrance. Note that the regulations, their implementation, and exceptions and waivers, may change frequently and without notice.

W

WEBSITES

www.ayia-napa.net – useful Agia Napa general site.
www.cyprus.com – tourism guide covering the whole island.
www.cyprus.gov.cy – the official government information site.
www.cyprushotelassociation.org – comprehensive hotel listing, but no reviews.
www.cyprus-mail.com – website of the *Cyprus Mail* newspaper.
www.cyprus-restaurants.com – a good eating-out listing for both North and South Cyprus.
www.cyprusweekly.com.cy – the website of the *Cyprus Weekly* newspaper.
www.kypros.org – a general-information website.
www.northcyprusonline.com – tourism site covering the North.
www.windowoncyprus.com – good general site covering the South.

Y

YOUTH HOSTELS

Cyprus has just one youth hostel, near Agios Lazaros in Larnaka at 27 Odos Nikolaou Rossou, tel: 2462 1188.

Recommended Hotels

Most hotels in Cyprus are in resorts and aimed at pre-booked holiday-makers. Although there are many fine hotels, there is a shortage of small hotels with unique character.

Resort hotels rule along the southern coastline: around Larnaka Bay, between Limassol and Amathous, and between between Agia Napa and Protaras-Pernera. There is a broader range of hotel types in the towns of Larnaka and Limassol. The western coastline has a wide range of choice, from spa-resort hotels in Pafos and at Coral Bay, to small, homely places around Lakki and Polis.

Inland, the capital Nicosia has a good range of hotels, from business-orientated to boutique and independent. The choice is greater in South Nicosia than in North Nicosia. Although there are relatively few hotels in the Troodos Mountains, what is available is varied and interesting.

In Northern Cyprus hotels are up to 30 percent cheaper than their Southern counterparts. The hotels in and around Keryneia (Girne) are likely to have more character than the resort hotels in and around Famagusta (Ammochostos/Gazimağusa).

€€€€€	over 240 euros
€€€€	180–240 euros
€€€	120–180 euros
€€	60–120 euros
€	under 60 euros

SOUTHERN CYPRUS

NICOSIA

Averof €€ *19 Odos Averof, tel: 2277 3447, fax: 2277 3411, www. averof.com.cy.* This friendly, family-run two-star hotel is one of the best budget choices in Nicosia, a 15-minute walk from the old town walls and a 10-minute walk from the municipal pool. 25 rooms.

Classic €€ *94 Odos Rigainis, tel: 2266 4006, fax: 2267 0072, www.classic.com.cy.* This hotel lies just within the city walls near

Pafos Gate, a 10-minute walk from the Ledra Palace Hotel checkpoint. It has small but comfortable bedrooms, a lively cocktail bar, an excellent restaurant (Fifty-Nine Knives, *see page 104*) and a small but well-equipped gym, all of which belie its two-star rating. 57 rooms.

Cyprus Hilton €€€€€ *Leoforos Archiepiskopou Makariou III, tel: 2237 7777, fax: 2237 7788, www.hilton.com.* This five-star hotel is in a relatively quiet setting back from the main road, a 15-minute drive from the old town. It has three restaurants and excellent sports facilities, including a pool, tennis courts and health club. 298 rooms.

Holiday Inn Nicosia €€€ *70 Odos Rigainis, tel: 2271 2712, fax: 2267 3337, www.ichotelsgroup.com.* This four-star hotel features its own Japanese restaurant *(see page 104)*, swimming pool and health club, and has a good location just within the city walls close to Plateia Eleftherias. 140 rooms.

Sky €€ *7c Odos Solonos, tel: 2266 6880, fax: 2267 2096, www.skyhotel.ws.* A good bet for budget travellers in the capital, the Sky won't win any modern-design awards, but the rooms are nicely furnished and well taken care of, and have small balconies. The central location inside the Venetian Walls, just off Plateia Eleftherias is a big plus, as is the associated Fanous Lebanese restaurant. 24 rooms.

LARNAKA

Flamingo Beach €€ *152 Leoforos Piyale Paşa, tel: 2482 8224, fax: 2465 6564, www.flamingobeachhotel.com.* This family-run, three-star seafront hotel lies on the southern edge of town, just after the fort, at the start of Mackenzie Beach. All rooms have a seaview balcony. Rooftop pool. 64 rooms.

Golden Bay €€€€€ *Larnaka–Dekeleia road, tel: 2464 5444, fax: 2464 5451, www.goldenbay.com.cy.* This five-star beachfront hotel lies 8km (5 miles) east of town and is set in landscaped gardens.

Rooms and suites are of a high standard. Excellent leisure and health facilities include an outdoor Jacuzzi. 193 rooms.

Sandy Beach €€ *Larnaka–Dekeleia road, tel: 2464 6333, fax: 2464 6900, www.sandybeachhotel.com.cy.* Friendly four-star beachfront hotel on Larnaka Bay, 7km (4 miles) east of town, with tavernas, bars and restaurants within walking distance. Indoor and outdoor swimming pools, good health club and gym. 195 rooms.

Sun Hall €€€ *6 Leoforos Athinou, tel: 2465 3341, fax: 2465 2717, www.aquasolhotels.com.* A four-star hotel right in the centre of the action on the main Palm Tree Promenade, opposite the beach and marina. Facilities include a health club, gym and swimming pool. 112 rooms.

AGIA NAPA AND REGION

Asterias Beach €€ *Makronisos, Agia Napa, tel: 2372 1901, fax: 2372 2095, www.asteriashotels.com.* Set on the edge of town on the popular sandy beach of Makronisos, this well-equipped four-star hotel has its own swimming pool and tennis courts, and many other facilities. 198 rooms.

Grecian Park €€€€ *81 Odos Konnos, Konnos Bay, Protaras, tel: 2384 4000, fax: 2383 2870, www.grecianpark.com.* Located halfway between Agia Napa and Protaras, this five-star hotel enjoys a fine hilltop location overlooking the sandy Konnos Bay beach. It features luxurious public areas, a large free-form swimming pool and a grassy sunbathing terrace with excellent sea views. 239 rooms.

Louis Nausicaa Beach €€ *17 Odos Syttarkas, Protaras, tel: 2383 1160, fax: 2383 1519, www.louishotels.com.* These classy low-rise apartments enjoy a great location on a promontory overlooking beautiful Fig Tree Bay and the island's best sandy beaches. Accommodation is spacious, comfortable and stylish, with a whitewashed Mediterranean theme. 195 rooms.

LIMASSOL (LEMESOS)

Ajax €€€ *Corner of Odos Damon and Odos D. Nikolaou, Mesa Geitonia, tel: 2559 0000, fax: 2559 1222, www.ajaxhotel.com.* This modern four-star hotel is set between the tourist area of Potamos Germasogeias and the town centre, about 1km (½ mile) from the beach. Facilities include outdoor and indoor pools, floodlit tennis courts, a health club and a kids' club. 176 rooms.

Amathus Beach €€€€€ *Leoforos Amathous, tel: 2583 2000, fax: 2583 2540, www.amathus-hotels.com.* This five-star beachfront hotel set 9km (6 miles) east of the city centre has extensive landscaped grounds, a spa and wellness centre, and two swimming pools, one of which has underwater music. In summer, the hotel runs its own beachside fish taverna. 239 rooms.

Le Méridien Spa & Resort €€€€€ *Amathous, tel: 2586 2000, fax: 2563 4222, www.lemeridienlimassol.com.* A superb hotel 12km (7 miles) east of Limassol, set in its own spacious gardens and with a large free-form pool, the Méridien has 300m (1,000ft) of beach frontage. Rooms are spacious, all with large balconies, and equipped to the highest standards. 295 rooms.

TROODOS MOUNTAINS

Forest Park Hotel €€€ *Pano Platres, tel: 2542 1751, fax: 2542 1875, www.forestparkhotel.com.cy.* Nestling in its own forest, the four-star Forest Park offers many of the creature comforts of its beachside counterparts, including a heated outdoor pool and an indoor pool. It is within walking distance of Pano Platres village. 137 rooms.

Linos Inn €€ *34 Odos Palaias, Kakopetria, tel: 2292 3161, fax: 2292 3181, www.linos-inn.com.cy.* This beautifully restored group of old village houses offers a romantic and homely setting with lots of antique fittings and furnishings. Facilities include mini-bars and satellite TV, sauna and Jacuzzi, and an attractive traditional restaurant. 22 rooms.

Mountain Rose € *Pedoulas, tel: 2295 2727, fax: 2295 2555.* Set on one end of the main street, this modest hotel has a rustic look that is entirely appropriate to a mountain village. The rooms are plain but clean and offer the choice of a view at the front and peace and quiet at the back. The simple ground-floor restaurant is one of the few dining options in Pedoulas. 21 rooms.

PAFOS AND REGION

Alexander the Great €€€€ *Leoforos Poseidonos, Pafos, tel: 2696 5000, fax: 2696 5100, www.kanikahotels.com.* Located on the best stretch of town beach, this four-star hotel is close to all town centre activities. Sporting facilities include outdoor and indoor pools and tennis courts. Health and beauty club. 202 rooms.

Aliathon Holiday Village €€ *Leoforos Poseidonos, Kato Pafos, tel: 2696 4400, fax: 2696 4700, www.aliathonvillage.com.* Just 200m (700ft) from the beach, this attractive complex of bungalows and apartments, artfully designed to look like a Greek village, is set around a swimming pool and gardens. It has all the facilities of a large three- or four-star hotel, but on a smaller scale. 260 rooms and apartments.

Annabelle €€€€€ *Leoforos Poseidonos, Pafos, tel: 2688 5000, fax: 2694 5502, www.annabelle.com.cy.* This refined, luxury five-star beachfront hotel is in the centre of town overlooking the harbour. Attractive gardens surround the pool. Rooms are large and well-furnished. Good sports facilities and restaurant. 218 rooms.

Coral Beach €€€€€ *Coral Beach, tel: 2688 1000, fax: 2662 2930, www.coral.com.cy.* Some 12km (7 miles) north of Pafos, this highly rated luxury five-star resort is the perfect place to escape the bustle of town, with lush landscaped gardens that open directly onto a sandy beach. There is an extensive range of leisure facilities, including a health and beauty spa, floodlit tennis courts, an archery range and an innovative arts and crafts centre, where guests can try their hand at glass painting, pottery and ceramic painting. 421 rooms.

Cynthiana Beach €€€ *Kisonerga, tel: 2693 3900, fax: 2694 4648, www.cynthianahotel.com.* This three-star beachfront hotel is about 8km (5 miles) west of town on a headland, in large landscaped gardens flanked by banana plantations, with a sandy beach immediately below. Indoor and outdoor swimming pools, tennis courts and other sports facilities. 230 rooms.

Kiniras €€ *91 Leoforos Archiepiskopou Makariou III, tel: 2694 1604, fax: 2694 2176, www.kiniras.cy.net.* If you don't need a beachfront setting or four-star luxury, this charming small hotel is a traditional 70-year-old house with public areas beautifully decorated in rustic style. Rooms are plain but comfortable. Although it's on the upper town's main street, it is quiet at night. No pool but the municipal baths are just 200m (220yds) away. 18 rooms.

Riu Cypria Resort €€€ *Leoforos Poseidonos, Geroskipou, tel: 2688 2688, fax: 2688 2690, www.riu.com.* This smart four-star hotel 3km (2 miles) east of the harbour features a little more style and character than other comparable Pafos accommodation. Extensive palm-shaded gardens surround the pool and lead directly onto the beach. 40 rooms.

Roman €€ *Odos Agiou Lamprianou, tel: 2694 5411, fax: 2694 6834, www.romanhotel.com.cy.* Perfectly positioned, just 1km (½ mile) from the town centre and a five-minute walk from the beach, the three-star Roman has the look of an ancient monument from the outside, while the interior is a daring and fanciful exercise in ancient Roman-style décor with bold wall paintings, colourful mosaics and other 'Roman' paraphernalia. Small swimming pool. 87 rooms.

Vasilias Nikoklis Inn €€€ *Nikokleia village, tel: 2643 2211, fax: 2643 2467, www.vasilias.nikoklis.com.* About as far away in spirit as you can get from the big resort hotels in Pafos – and not so close in terms of distance either – this is a lovingly restored, and expanded rustic stonebuilt inn that perfectly complements its location in the Diarizos valley just outside the village. The restaurant with tables under a pergola is as noteworthy as the accommodation. 8 rooms.

NORTHERN CYPRUS

NORTHERN NICOSIA (LEFKOŞA)

Saray €€ *Atatürk Meydanı, tel: 228 3115, fax: 228 4408, email: saray.hotel@superonline.com.* Dating from the 1950s – and looking it, despite refurbishment – this is nevertheless the top hotel in the Turkish-Cypriot part of the capital. It offsets its somewhat undistinguished character with reasonable comfort, a fine position on the northern sector's main square, and a rooftop bar and restaurant with a great view over the city. 72 rooms.

KERYNEIA (GIRNE)

British Hotel € *Kordonboyu, tel: 815 2453, fax: 815 2772, www.britishhotelcyprus.com.* The kind of more-than-decent small hotel with character that Cyprus, North or South, doesn't have anything like enough of, the British has a superb location overlooking Keryneia's handsome harbour. Most room have balconies. Breakfast on the terrace is a treat all by itself. 18 rooms.

Dome €€€ *Kordonboyu, tel: 815 2454, fax: 815 2772, www.hotel dome.com.* This stylish waterfront hotel near the harbour still retains some of its colonial-heyday cachet, despite the casino that has been added to boost revenues. Its cosmopolitan air is complemented by well-equipped rooms, many of them with views, and a fair restaurant that serves both Turkish and international cuisine. 160 rooms.

FAMAGUSTA (GAZIMAĞUSA)

Bilfer Palm Beach €€€ *Deve Limanı, tel: 366 2000, fax: 366 2002, www.northernpalmbeach.com.* Pastel-toned and graceful, the hotel stands right up against Famagusta's abandoned and derelict former Greek Cypriot suburb, Varosha. The Palm Beach resolutely averts its eyes, focusing instead on its own chic interior and de luxe lifestyle, and on the superb beach located out front. 108 rooms.

INDEX

Berlitz pocket guide

Cyprus

Eighth Edition 2011

Written by Paul Murphy
Updated by George McDonald
Edited by Alex Knights
Series Editor: Tony Halliday

Photography credits
Caroline Jones 4–5, 5tc, 9, 12, 15, 16, 19, 20, 26, 28, 30, 34, 35, 40, 43, 44, 50, 52, 53, 55, 57, 58, 59, 60, 61, 63, 64, 68, 71, 72, 73, 76, 78, 82, 84, 86, 88, 94, 97; Jon Davison 24, 36; istockphoto 4tl, 4tc, 4br; 46; Britta Jaschinski 5br; LOOK-foto/photolibrary 5bl; Paul Murphy 8, 10, 17, 38, 48, 54, 62, 69, 91, 102; Richard Nowitz 5tr; Franco Pecchio 4bl; George Taylor 22, 32, 39, 41, 42, 49, 66, 75, 80, 81, 83, 92, 101; Bill Wassman 98.

Cover picture: Robert Harding

Contact us

At Berlitz we strive to keep our guides as accurate and up to date as possible, but if you find anything that has changed, or if you have any suggestions on ways to improve this guide, then we would be delighted to hear from you.

Berlitz Publishing, PO Box 7910, London SE1 1WE, England
email: berlitz@apaguide.co.uk
www.berlitzpublishing.com